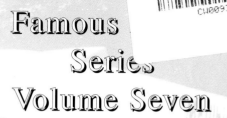

Famous
Series
Volume Seven

THE
MR. WHIPPY
STORY

Steve Tillyer

WALL'S

Nostalgia Road Publications

Wall's

Mr. Whippy

CONTENTS

The **Famous Fleets** Series ™

is produced under licence by

Nostalgia Road Publications Ltd.

Unit 6, Chancel Place

Shap Road Industrial Estate, Kendal LA9 6NZ

Tel. 01539 738832 - Fax: 01539 730075

designed and published by
Trans-Pennine Publishing Ltd.
PO Box 10, Appleby-in-Westmorland, Cumbria, CA16 6FA
Tel. 017683 51053 Fax. 017683 53558
e-mail: admin@transpenninepublishing.co.uk

and printed by
Kent Valley Colour Printers Ltd.
Kendal, Cumbria
01539 741344

© Trans-Pennine Publishing Ltd. 2003
Photographs: Author's collection or as credited

Front Cover: *Taken in Australia Circa 1965 Don Swaffer (left) and Bill Kendell pose for the camera. Photo Peter Hopkins*

Rear Cover Top: *This pretty Electrofreeze Bedford CA is probably a very early example circa 1965. Photo Unilever.*

Rear Cover Bottom: *This Mercedes 300D at the new Rockingham Motor Speedway, shows the latest Wall's Heart-brand livery. Photo Steve Tillyer.*

Title Page: *This Morrison CF Bedford is clearly branded as Mr. Whippy; however, although the van is in Wall's colours and bodywork transfers it is not necessarily selling Wall's products. This and many other variations using the Mr. Whippy name were not uncommon and certainly became a difficult problem for the manufacturers to police. Photo Andy Ballisat*

This Page: *This late 1980s postcard shows a Morrison-built Bedford CF2 on East Hill, St Leonards-On-Sea, which was owned by PWW Ice Cream Supplies. The grill on the side and rear indicates that this van used a generator to power a rear mounted ice cream machine. Photo Robin Weir*

FOREWORD

Mr.Whippy was a key commercial building block that helped drive Wall's into its position as the biggest branded ice cream manufacturer in the UK.

As this book goes to print, it is 40 years since Wall's acquired part-ownership in the Mr.Whippy brand and many of us remember growing up with Mr.Whippy bringing soft ice cream right to the streets where we played as children. Wall's continues to bring the very best ice cream to people in the UK to enjoy wherever they are:- - Walls now have 14 of the top 20 branks in the UK.

Mr.Whippy was designed originally to bring ice cream to people at their front doors and Wall's continues to do just that, in many different ways: we still use the most up to date technology to ensure that consumers can find a Wall's ice cream that is made and sold in the most convenient and hygienic way possible. Mr.Whippy played a fundamental part in ice cream's success story, as did the people originally associated with Mr.Whippy and those who continue to bring the best ice cream to our consumers through mobiling.

James Hill and *Gaby Vreeken*
Unilever Ice Cream & Frozen Food

INTRODUCTION

As our title states, this is a book about "Mr. Whippy". Now! Many readers may be forgiven for thinking that this was all about 'soft ice cream' rather than that famous brand name. The term Mr. Whippy has long become a generic term for soft ice cream. Generic terminology is obviously not a new phenomenon and in many ways is a form of flattery. How many of us refer to our vacuum cleaner as a 'Hoover' or a ballpoint pen as a 'Biro' or indeed a spa bath as a 'Jacuzzi'?

However, our subject matter here, deals with that famous brand found on those ubiquitous pink and cream vans that were much loved by the children of the 1960s and '70s. Following the difficult years of the mid-1950s, 1959 was regarded by many as the time that Britain finally broke free from its post-war austerity. Cliff Richard was about to have his first number one, General Motors had just launched its outrageous 'Pink Cadillac' and the streets of Britain were about to get ice cream "American Style".

Above: *In a promotion by Revlon Cosmetics, Mr. Whippy vans line-up outside Myers Department Store in Melbourne's city centre. Each van carried a pretty Revlon girl, which the drivers considered to be a welcome change.* Photo Bob Staff,

Ice cream had always been a favourite of the rich and famous but its general availability to the masses through mobile sales was only really developed between the two World Wars. It was in London in 1922 that T Wall & Sons launched their now famous 'stop me and buy one' trikes. This proved an immediate success and by the outbreak of World War II the "Wallsie trikes" were a common sight up and down the country.

With an estimated fleet of 8,500 'trikes', mobiling had arrived and the people loved it! It is therefore fitting that the story of 'Mr. Whippy' is well and truly woven into the fabric of Wall's ice cream, the largest, and commercially most successful ice cream company in the UK to date.

The cessation of hostilities in 1945 saw the gradual re-introduction of mobiling and sales slowly gathered momentum throughout those post-war austerity years. As rationing gave way to the consumer boom of a 'live now, pay later' Britain, an explosion of mobiling activity took full advantage of the newly acquired surplus income being enjoyed by a much wider section of society.

The Mr.Whippy story told here is born out of the success of *The Mister Softee* story launched at the Ice Cream Alliance exhibition at Harrogate in November 2000. It became obvious from the response received to this Nostalgia Road' book, that we had to bring to fruition this equally important piece of mobiling history. The 'Mr Whippy' story simply had to be told.

Some 44 years on from their introduction, the brands of Mr.Whippy (and indeed Mister Softee) are still household names, synonymous with 'soft ice cream'. It is therefore difficult to understand why their respective owners no longer market these famous brands; but in the meantime read on and enjoy a nostalgic trip down Mobiling Memory Lane. Yippee! - It's Mr Whippy!

Steve Tillyer,   Laxton, Northants. October 2003

Top Right: *Taken in Queensland Australia in the mid-1960s, the driver here is Len Welbeloved who later became a manager for Mr.Whippy Pty Ltd. Upwards of two hundred of these Electrofreeze Commer/Karrier vans were shipped to Australia, Tasmania and New Zealand during the mid-sixties. The vans seen here used the Carpigiani machine, but other machines were considered. The Sweden-Freeze, which was the preferred choice for Mister Softee, was at one stage tried by Mr.Whippy. Unfortunately the staff at Mr.Whippy could not get the Sweden to work properly as the ice cream was serving far too soft. A Sweden engineer was called in, and after several tests, he concluded that the mix was not suited to the machine. Some Mister Softee mix was then obtained and put through its paces in the Sweden. The result was fine every time a cornet was pulled and Mr.Whippy therefore decided to stay with Carpigiani. Photo Val Welbeloved..*

Bottom Right: *This and many other such adverts were placed in the 'Ice Cream Alliance' journal during the formative years of Mr.Whippy. Not only were Mr.Whippy trying to attract individual drivers, but also the fleet operator willing to join the Mr.Whippy club as a franchised agent. The company launched its first six vans in Birmingham during the spring of 1959, with the Head Office being in Leamington Spa where Dominic Facchino and his wife lived. Note the early ice cream machine, which pre-dates the 'Doppia' van model. As well as trade advertising Mr.Whippy also placed adverts in the local press when a new depot was opened. There was also a limited amount of TV advertising on a regional basis. Photo Ice Cream Alliance*

Mr. Whippy gives a few hard facts...

about SOFT ICE CREAM

Whether you make and sell it on the spot in a Mr. Whippy mobile dairy van or from your shop, soft ice cream has come to stay! Any of the large stores selling both types of ice cream will tell you that soft ice cream sales are by far the highest and now—thanks to Mr. Whippy—you too can share in this success! Write NOW for further particulars---you will be under no obligation.

MR. WHIPPY (Soft Freeze) LTD.
61, WARWICK STREET, LEAMINGTON SPA

16   ICE CREAM & FROZEN CONFECTIONERY. OCTOBER, 1960

THE EARLY YEARS

As with many ice cream stories, it will come as no surprise to find that this one has its roots in 19th century Italy. A young man called Enrico Facchino and his wife Angela Maria from a town called Sora just south of Rome in the province of Frosinone decided to start a new life and chose Britain as their new home in the late 1890s.

The two settled in Birmingham, where Enrico initially carried on his trade of shoemaking. It wasn't long before the family began to expand with the arrival of Anthony followed by a further three boys and six girls. Enrico was a hard worker with ambition and before long he opened a shop selling general goods and imported Italian foods and wine, which he sold to the local Italian community. Things were a whole lot different in those days, as Enrico used to have to go to the docks in London and Hull to acquire his produce.

Above: *This Electrofreeze CA Bedford was first registered to Tartaglia's in 1965. Mike Allen of Tartaglia's says it was a prototype van with much of the panelwork made of aluminium, unlike the later all GRP-bodied models.* Photo Unilever

It wasn't long before he and Angela Maria started to manufacture their own ice cream, which they traded from handcarts. Subsequently a horse and cart was bought, which allowed Enrico to trade further afield, while the older children took out the handcarts. So ice cream soon became an important part of the family business. The ice cream trade in Birmingham was expanding, and Enrico saw an opportunity to offer manufacturing facilities to local Italians who wanted to produce their own ice cream products. With the hostilities of World War I fading, Enrico decided to open what can only be described as a 'communal' ice cream factory.

Top Right: *Enrico and his wife Angela Maria established the family business in Birmingham during the early part of the 20th century. Their shop in 'Little Italy' specialised in selling Italian goods and produce, and then later on their own ice cream; ice cream would then develop into a significant part of their business.* Photo Peter Hopkins

Centre Right: *This picture was taken in 1908 and it shows a Devoti's Italian Ice cream cart in Birmingham. It is included in this book on Mr.Whippy because the expanding Italian ice cream businesses prompted Enrico Facchino to open a small factory in the city just after World War I. His new factory offered the growing Italian community the opportunity to produce their own ice cream.* Photo Peter Hopkins.

Bottom Right: *The Facchino biscuit factory had beautiful gardens, which were a particular source of pride and joy to its owner Enrico Facchino.* Photo Peter Hopkins.

A dozen or so local Italians leased his premises and equipment where they made their own ice cream. At this time Enrico's wife would run the shop with their eldest daughter Mary. Times were hard so starting work at 4am was quite normal, as they had to make the ice cream before starting work in the shop. It was a slow process in those old ice and salt freezers, so an early start ensured that plenty of ice cream would be ready for Enrico, along with his sons and daughters, to trade.

In the Birmingham area known as 'little Italy there were numerous ice cream traders. By this time the use of biscuit cones and wafers had become commonplace, and as such, gave rise to a new opportunity. Enrico, along with his eldest son Anthony, saw the possibilities of producing ice cream biscuits, cones and wafers for their friends and rivals alike.

This idea took shape in the purchase of a factory in Bradford Street, and was the start of what was arguably to become one of the largest producers of ice cream biscuits in the country. Enrico's second eldest son, Paul, became the factory engineer. He was mainly self-taught and was responsible for installing and maintaining the wafer and cone machines. He then went on to install an automated production line that radically increased productivity and reduced wastage.

Enter Dominic Facchino, Enrico's third eldest son and the man who was later to become the driving force behind the launch of Mr Whippy. Dominic was sent out on the road (with the company's first salesman, Walter Relph) to promote and sell their products. At this time Enrico had entrusted the administration and direction of the company to Anthony. However, one suspects that on a day-to-day basis, this was far from the truth, with Enrico still being the power behind the throne.

The company became so successful that they soon outgrew the Bradford Street factory and had to look for much larger premises. Anthony took on the main responsibility for this and eventually found a suitable site in the Ward End district of Birmingham. It was then decided that the best way forward was for the company to design and build its own factory to meet their growing needs.

Anthony, along with his brothers and of course Enrico, then planned the building of their new factory. The new factory, which opened in 1925 was immediately fronted by beautiful gardens (inspired by the 'governor' Enrico) and soon became a local landmark. A new limited company was formed at this time under the name of Facchino's Purity Biscuits Ltd with the four Facchino brothers as directors. Anthony was the Managing Director, Paul was the Works Director, Dominic was Sales Director and Joseph Production Director.

Much later the company developed an ice cream powder, which when combined with water, produced an ice cream mix. This product was marketed through a new company called Meddocream Ltd. In the 1950s National Ice Cream manufacturers, such as Wall's, Lyons. Eldorado and Neilsons, were perceived to be a threat to the existence of the localised manufacturers who were often small family firms, so Dominic Facchino devised a scheme known as 'The Meddocream Scheme'.

Selected local ice cream manufacturers were invited to join the scheme, which was marketed under the Meddocream trade name. The powder was packed in 28lb tins and this enabled customers to manufacture 'Freshly Made Ice Cream' from their own premises. More importantly, it allowed the small producer to comply with the Ice Cream Heat Treatment Regulations that had been introduced in 1948. The powdered mix eventually gave way to a freshly manufactured mix made from raw materials to a recipe formulated by Meddocream.

In 1956, the growth of the Meddocream organisation, prompted a successful takeover bid by Neilsons, owned by the Canadian entrepreneur Garfield Weston. Dominic Facchino remained and was appointed as Managing Director of the subsidiary, but Anthony Facchino continued in the same role at the biscuit company, which was later brought under the Garfield Weston umbrella.

As a result of his experience in the family business, Dominic, in particular, had always been aware of the popularity of freshly made soft ice cream and indeed, the Facchino biscuit company had already developed a special XL cone for soft serve ice cream. Facchino's supplied approximately half the 730 or so Woolworth stores in the UK, and for those who are not old enough to remember, nearly all these stores sold ice cream. Some stores, had two ice cream selling points, one for hard and one for soft ice cream, with the latter being produced in vertical batch freezers. In this situation, the supply of XL cones was always four to five times greater than hard ice cream cones, thus proving the popularity of soft ice cream.

Legend has it that in the late 1950s, Dominic would spend a lot of his time in ice cream queues in and around the Birmingham area, observing, listening and sampling ice cream. Whether or not this is true, he certainly knew what the public wanted, and that was freshly made soft serve ice cream. However, little did he know that within a few years, he would be dubbed by some as 'The Ice Cream King'.

Below: *All looking very smart in this publicity shot for the brochure called 'Frozen Assets'. By the time it was published in the late summer of 1962 the company, (which had been launched on a shoestring), had grown to become a major player in the ice cream business. By the end of its third year of trading, Mr.Whippy had certainly come of age, with 735 vehicles operating throughout Britain. It had also built its own 'state of the art' ice cream factory and had a 50% share in the Southampton-based vehicle production facility. Now riding high, a public floatation was considered, but shelved when a take-over by the Forte Group looked the better option. As 1962 came to a close, Dominic Facchino had taken the Mr.Whippy brand from a £100 company in 1959, to being part of the 'Forte empire' and in doing so had made himself a millionaire.*
Photo Peter Hopkins

Meddocream Ltd
ICE CREAM SAMPLES

BIRTH OF A BRAND

Although Dominic Facchino continued to work for Garfield Weston at a senior management level, he was an entrepreneur at heart, and I'm sure, longed to be back paddling his own canoe. In 1958 Dominic visited America. It's not known why he was there, but he certainly had meetings with the Conway Brothers, the founders of the Mister Softee operation. The story goes that whilst there he saw one of the Conway brother's ground breaking 'ice cream factories on wheels'. The impact of these 'trucks' on Dominic was such that he immediately entered into negotiations with the Conways in an effort to secure the Mister Softee franchise in the UK. This was not to be, as the Conways were more impressed by the stature of the Lyons/Smiths collaboration (see *The Mister Softee Story*), which subsequently acquired the UK Softee franchise.

Undeterred, Dominic returned home to the UK secure in his mind that mobile soft ice cream had immense possibilities and therefore decided to go it alone. By late 1958 the Mr.Whippy concept was formulated. He gave up his lucrative £5,000-a-year job with Nielson and formed a £100 company based in Leamington Spa. Joining him on the payroll were his two sisters, Philomena and Stella, along with a trusted colleague, friend and nephew Peter Hopkins, who also gave up a well-paid job to join the embryonic Mr.Whippy team.

It was therefore decided that the best way forward was to set up a pilot scheme of six vans and monitor the public's response to the 'new' ice cream factories on wheels'.

Above: *From his experience at Facchino Biscuits, Meddocream and Neilsons Ice Cream, Dominic Facchino went on to establish a brand that has simply become part of our language. The young man standing eighth from right is Peter Hopkins, who can best be described as Dominic's right hand man, particularly during the formative years at Mr.Whippy. Much of this book could not have been written without Peter's superb memory and his collection of archive material.*

Although confidence in the Mr.Whippy concept was high, it was nevertheless a gamble when considering that five or six hard vans could be purchased for the cost of one Mr.Whippy van.

Dominic decided to use an advertising agency (Longley's & Hoffman of Birmingham) to help create a professional and uniquely identifiable image. Dominic worked closely with Mr L A Binns, from the agency to eventually arrive at the now famous Mr.Whippy brand, although the prototype vans in the pilot scheme were in a much simpler livery. They knew that the Mister Softee vehicles (soon to be launched) would be in blue and white livery, so pink and cream became an obvious choice for Dominic, who wanted to create a powerful and uncluttered image to rival the American Mister Softee brand. The now familiar Greensleeve's chime was adopted along with a smiling faced Mr.Whippy man logo. The Mr.Whippy man wore a Henry VIII style bonnet and was given 'dancing feet'; the end result being an instantly identifiable brand image to rival the American Softee brand.

The first vans were introduced in April 1959 and worked from the newly acquired premises in Burbury Street, in the Lozells area of Birmingham. The first van was driven by Ted Vaughan who later became a senior supervisor! A new company (Mr.Whippy Ltd) was formed on the 1st April 1959 with four Facchino directors, Dominic, Paul, Joseph and Stella. A sister operation of six Mr.Whippy vans soon followed in Hounslow, West London, run by Ernest Pacitto, a business associate of Dominic.

Pacitto already operated vans under the Mylo's brand in West London and Southend-on-Sea and he also produced the ice cream mix for the London pilot scheme. He was also the man responsible for negotiating with Carpigiani of Bolognia to produce a van freezer for Mr.Whippy. This move proved to be a key element in the operational success of Mr.Whippy and also established the reputation of this Italian manufacturer as a leader in mobile soft-serve machines.

Above: *This photo of an MTS-built van for Mylo's may have been taken prior to the 1960 Commercial Motor Show. Mylo's operated the first Mr.Whippy vans in London.* Photo Peter Carverhill

In fact, Ernest Pacitto held the Carpigiani franchise for several years until it was taken over by Morrisons. Mobilers now take the popular Carpigiani machine for granted. However, in 1958, no soft ice cream machines were specifically designed for vans. In fact, the Sweden Freeze machines used in the early years by Mister Softee were simply shop models with the wheels removed. It is interesting to note the lack of local and national media coverage during the launch of Mr.Whippy. This apparently was a deliberate strategy, as Dominic felt that by keeping his head down he would gain valuable time to establish Mr.Whippy before the big firms caught on. However, some limited TV advertising was used to good effect in Birmingham during the spring and early summer of 1959.

It should be noted that Lyons were ahead of the game with their involvement in the launch of Mister Softee a month earlier. Dominic's fear of the 'big boys' was surely aimed at the other big players such as Wall's, who fortunately for Dominic demonstrated an apparent total disinterest to soft ice cream. It's fair to say that this was quite common at the time, as many in the trade were extremely sceptical about the future of soft ice cream mobiling due to its high capital and maintenance costs. Mr.Whippy and Mister Softee were about to prove them all wrong!

Some of the early operators were far-sighted and continued to expand with Mr.Whippy. They proved that despite the high capital costs involved, soft ice cream mobiling was a lucrative business and here to stay, Yet, as the problems of the post launch period became resolved, new franchisees were brought on-line for the 1960 season. Ice cream operators such as Ken Reynolds of Grays, Harry Williams of Barking, George Cooper of Welwyn Garden City, Leo Di Mascio of Mitcham, and John Di Mascio of Erith were all in the vanguard of soft ice cream mobiling.

The problems encountered in those early days by Mister Softee were also mirrored at Mr.Whippy, mainly because nobody had experience of the new technology and a steep and sometimes painful learning curve was the order of the day. For example, the early industrial Coventry Victor powered generators overheated badly and the generator compartment was poorly designed with inadequate ventilation. Drivers often forgot to switch from TVO to petrol before shutdown, which meant the generator would not start the next day. The new Carpigiani machines were expensive and well built, but novice (and probably poorly trained) salesmen could cause expensive repairs to be needed.

.From the outset, the rapid growth of Mr.Whippy was achieved through franchising the operation and in this concept Dominic would call on his experience at Meddocream and Neilsons. However, the emerging profitability of fleet operations meant that the business would now grow on two fronts, with company-owned vehicle numbers just exceeding the franchised operators by the end of the third year of trading. Although Mr.Whippy got off to a slower start than Mister Softee, a respectable 735 vehicles were in operation nationwide by the end of 1962, by which time Mr.Whippy had come of age and was emerging as a household name. The brand subsequently became strong enough to silently slip into the English language.

Top Right: *Through into the mid-1960s, Warwick House, Leamington Spa was the hub of Mr.Whippy's operations.* Photo Peter Hopkins

Centre Right: *Dominic Facchino was the driving force behind the launch and subsequent success of Mr.Whippy. He retired to the Channel Islands and sadly died before this book could be published.* Photo Peter Hopkins.

Bottom Right: *In 1962 Mr.Whippy built a state of the art ice cream factory in Basildon in Essex. The plant was run by Mr A E Pelosi.* Photo Peter Hopkins

COACH-BUILT VANS

The first Whippy vans were built on Commer/Karrier BF model forward-control 30cwt chassis by the coachbuilders, MTS of Feltham, West London. The ill-fated Coventry Victor-powered generator was soon replaced by an industrial version of a Ford Consul 1703cc engine, engineered by Stan Buchan and his team at AC Morrison Engineers of Southampton. However generator compartments need good ventilation and after the early teething troubles, a new generator compartment was soon designed.

To ensure continuity of supply, MTS coachbuilders were quickly taken over by Dominic Facchino and Ernest Pacitto for the sole purpose of building soft ice cream vans. Like Mister Softee vans (built by Smiths) these vans were extremely expensive, but not exclusive to Mr.Whippy franchise holders. A fully fitted Commer would set an operator back a cool £3,400 or a slightly reduced price of £3,200 if you were a Whippy franchise holder. As orders for Whippy vans increased it is understood that a small number of bodies were also constructed (with detailed differences) by Bonnalacks of Basildon, Essex.

Weighing in at well over three tons, the completed vans had features that arguably made them better to operate than those Commers built by Smiths of Gateshead for Mister Softee. Unlike Softee vans, the driving seat swivelled clockwise (via a foot-operated pedal), which allowed the driver easy access to the serving area. This avoided much swearing and personal injury as it wasn't necessary to climb over the hand brake and gear lever. Whippy vans also had one floor to roof side-opening door in the serving area, and this made life so much easier for washing out the vehicle and loading and unloading stock. An added benefit on later models was the ability to secure this door to the rear bodywork when fully open. This was a boon when pitching up on those hot summer days. However, taller drivers would no doubt have been envious of the extra headroom afforded to Mister Softee drivers.

Top Right: *This rather poor quality photograph was taken in Birmingham in 1959, and shows one of the first Mr.Whippy Commer vans built by MTS. These prototype vans had the Coventry Victor TVO engined generator sets, which badly overheated. The forward-hinged side-door, would later become rear-hinged to allow the door to fasten to the rear panel in the open position.* Photo Ice Cream Alliance

Centre Right: *During the rapid expansion of Mr.Whippy, Bonallack & Sons of Basildon in Essex were asked to build Mr.Whippy vans to the same specification and design as the MTS/Electrofreeze vehicles.* Photo Ice Cream Alliance.

Bottom Right: *The MkIII version shown here was the most space efficient, but lost the handy side-opening door. However, the new sliding window did afford the operator the choice of serving from both sides of the van.* Photo Bob Staff.

Arguably Mr.Whippy vans were better served by their larger 12.5kva, three phase (415 volt) generators. The extra 5kva of power, compared to Softee vans, allowed the use of a twin (Dopia), or latterly in some cases, two single (Singola) Carpigiani machines. The most commonly used generator power unit was Ford's robust 1703cc industrial version of the Consul/Zephyr engine, which at 1500rpm, ran 300 rpm slower than a Softee generator and therefore just a touch quieter. However it wasn't long before the twin machines were dropped, in favour of a single pump-fed machine, which allowed the smaller and cheaper (7.5kva Ford 102E side valve) generator sets to be fitted.

The new pump-fed machines were capable of producing more ice cream per hour than the earlier drip-fed models and kept up well with long queues. This reduced the overall weight and therefore allowed the use of the 12" shorter (and cheaper) 20cwt Commer Karrier chassis, which in turn significantly reduced the 'on-the-road cost' to a figure in the region of £2,500. However, by moving the Carpigiani ice cream machine a few inches forward into the driver's compartment, little useable space was lost by this 12" reduction in chassis length. In fact most drivers said that the new and lighter vehicles were better to drive.

Yet this model was only to be a stop-gap measure as Buchan and his team had taken over Mr.Whippy van production with a newly formed company called Electrofreeze (Equipments) Ltd. They soon realised that internal space could be much better utilised within the 1-ton chassis models. A new layout was conceived for 1962 and a prototype vehicle was designed, with a pre-production model being built by 'Piccador' the neighbouring Southampton builder of Tonibell vans. For some reason it did not go to Mr.Whippy, but to a Bristol mobiler, Colin Tarr. The upper space in the generator compartment was now incorporated into the main interior of the van, and for the first time, a rear window was introduced. The single 'clock-face' Carpigiani was now located over the generator facing forward, with the freezer and chiller in the place where the machine previously sat. This new configuration not only increased useable internal space and lightened the load on the front axle, but also gave the interior a more spacious feel and rearward visibility.

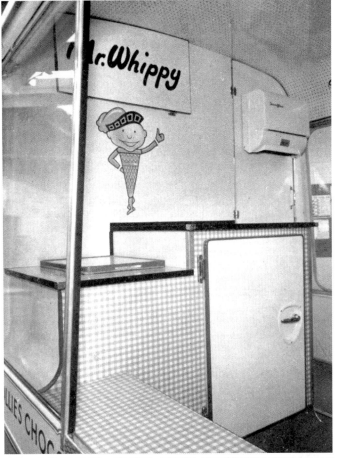

Top Left: *This period shot shows the interior of the MkIII model designed by Electrofreeze. The roof lining was in painted pegboard with blue gingham Formica surfaces. The white walls were made from Swedish Royal Board.* Photo Peter Hopkins

Bottom Left: *From 'Day One', regular advertising in the trade press ensured that Mr. Whippy continued to raise its profile within the trade.* Photo Ice Cream Alliance.

Back in 1959, the prototype Commer/Karrier vans were fitted out with grey and white Formica surfaces, which later gave way to the now familiar blue and white gingham design. The interior roof lining was made from pegboard and the (white) wipe clean wall surfaces were made of Swedish 'Royal Board'. The gingham Formica surfaces were used throughout the production life of Mr. Whippy Commer/Karriers, which ended in 1965. It is said that the vans were fitted with two 10-gallon water tanks, one of which supplied hot water via a gravity fed (240volt) immersion heater. However, both of the author's two 1961-built examples have only one hot supply fitted.

The early drip-fed Carpigiani machines were capable of producing up to seven gallons of ice cream per hour with a modest 40 per cent overrun. This of course would have been a considerably lower air to mix ratio than the later pump-fed machines. The vans had a capacity of keeping up to 32-gallons of fresh mix chilled, while the non-holdover cabinet (freezer) was small by today's standards. Each van had two full-length internal fluorescent strip lights, and one external one over the serving window. This made Whippy vans very attractive at night, and quite useful when you consider that soft ice cream vans were so popular in those early years, that working profitably during the dark winter evenings was possible.

With the introduction of the third and final Commer model from Electrofreeze, the design team turned its attention to the development of a 15-cwt model on the popular Bedford CA chassis with prototypes on the road by 1965. These GRP bodied models had three distinctive body styles and were made from many individual GRP mouldings fabricated by Wincanton Engineering. These new models also dispensed with Bedford's steel front end and the heavy side-by-side 7.5kva generator set was said to have been carried over to the 15-cwt chassis. However, I have my doubts, as this would surely have pushed the on-the-road weight over its limit. The much lighter Onan generator was also known to have been fitted, and was probably the choice for production models.

It is understood that several other ways of powering the Carpigiani machine were tried, one of these being the use of a slave engine located in the generator compartment. A 'Veloce' water-cooled engine was employed to provide the motive power via electro-magnetic clutches, but this configuration, for some reason, was not developed further.

The introduction of Bedford's new CF model in 1969 came as rather a surprise to Electrofreeze, who had to quickly develop a new body for customers such as Mr. Whippy and Mister Softee. At this point the Electrofreeze Managing Director, Stan Buchan, considered a return to a traditional coachbuilt body.

14

However, Terry Newman convinced him that a one-piece glass-reinforced plastic (GRP) body was the way forward. The only proviso being that he had to produce a design that did not require an interior lining. Many in the trade have said that this resulted in producing the finest van of its day. The proof of the pudding is always in the eating, and today Morrison Electrofreeze bodies are still being removed and mounted onto newer chassis.

With the introduction of the CF model, Morrisons looked to the 'Direct Drive' system (invented by Bryan Whitby) as the only practical way of powering the ice cream equipment. A pulley-type electro-magnetic clutch was mounted on the vehicle's engine to supply the motive power. The machine stayed in the Morrisons preferred position at the rear of the vehicle, facing forward. This necessitated the use of an RDG (reverse drive gearbox) machine, which enabled the equipment to turn in the right direction. The driver would have a red lever, which when depressed lifted the engine's speed and activated a switch to engage the electro-magnetic clutches. Later on, a rear-facing, front-mounted machine was introduced, and therefore available to the fully franchised Wall's-Whippy operation.

There was one other important development at Morrison Electrofreeze and it is well worth a mention here. When Vauxhall-Bedford axed the CA chassis, it left the Southampton company with a significant stock of bodies that couldn't be mounted onto the new chassis. Enter the Morrisons patented 'Powerdrive' model built on a new chassis by Roach Trailers of Ower. Although Mr.Whippy did not purchase these new, some second-hand examples were believed to have found their way into Mr.Whippy livery.

This new model employed a power take-off from the gearbox via a 'Simplitrol' electro-magnetic clutch. This in turn drove a shaft and pulley arrangement to rotate the 12kva, 415volt generator in the rear. This was all activated via a secondary (ignition type) key on the dashboard. This arrangement, designed by Ted Maynard, fed power to the solenoid, (and magnetic clutch), which in turn engaged the engine's governor. The 1:1 gearing from the Ford 1600 cross-flow unit meant that the governor kept the engine speed to 1,500 rpm. Most other parts were sourced from the Ford Transit and this is the reason why many people think that the 'Powerdrive' has a Ford Transit chassis. Some of these unique vans have survived and two are still known to be working today.

Chassis type M44 RH showing governed Powerdrive Unit between engine and gearbox, driving 12 kVA alternator.

Top Right: *The line-up of pretty Electrofreeze CAs, is seen here at the 1968 Ice Cream Alliance exhibition at Buxton.* Photo Ice Cream Alliance

Centre Right: *This 1970s Morrison built Bedford CF has a one-piece GRP body with a direct drive system from the front engine to power the ice cream-making equipment.* Photo Andy Ballisat

Bottom Right: *The 'Powerdrive' is the only known vehicle chassis to have been commissioned by an ice cream coachbuilder.* Photo Peter Hopkins

EMPIRE BUILDING

With Mr. Whippy now firmly established, Dominic Facchino defined his companies' aims as:
1) The building and selling of ice cream vehicles.
2) Mr. Whippy as a franchised operation.
3) Company-owned Mr. Whippy fleet operations.

These were heady days for all involved in what was fast becoming an ice cream empire. Peter Hopkins, who can best be described as Dominic Facchino's right-hand-man in the early days, particularly remembers those early years of 'empire' building with great affection. 'Dominic Facchino was, in my opinion, a great man, who enthused us all with his vitality and vision for the future. It was of course hard work and long hours, but we did feel that we were part of something special, and that was quite exciting'.

Above: *This evocative picture was taken in Australia shortly after the successful launch of Mr. Whippy in 1962. Note the Sundae dispenser.* Photo Peter Hopkins.

Before too long Mr. Whippy entered a period of acquisitions, partnerships, and expansion through the formation of new companies. On the vehicle building side, Dominic was not completely happy with the way things were going at MTS in Feltham, and it's understood that there was a 'parting of the ways' between Mr Pacitto and Dominic. This answers the question as to why an MTS-built Commer was displayed in Mylo's livery at the 1960 Commercial Motor Show, rather than in Mr. Whippy livery.

Dominic soon approached Stan Buchan at Morrisons, to see if his company would be interested in taking over vehicle production. Stan Buchan, by all accounts, was enthusiastic and set up a meeting with himself, Dominic, and the Morrison Board of Directors in London.

The idea of ice cream van production did not fit neatly into Morrison's corporate plans, and according to Stan Buchan the proposal 'left them feeling cold', and as a result their answer was a resounding No! Dominic however, was not deterred by that decision and was obviously impressed by Stan Buchan; so at a subsequent private meeting, Dominic proposed that they jointly form a new company to design, build and equip ice cream vans. Stan (together with his partners Ted Maynard and Geoff Goodwin), agreed, and on the 26th July 1960, Electrofreeze (Equipments) Ltd was born with Mr.Whippy holding a 50% share. By the spring of 1961 with over 100 Mr.Whippy vans on the road and Facchino's involvement in numerous companies, it was felt that an umbrella company should be formed. On the 28th April 1961, Mr.Whippy (Holdings) Ltd was formed, with Mr.Whippy Ltd, Mr.Whippy (Softfreeze) Ltd, Mr.Whippy (Tyne) Ltd, Mr.Whippy (Scotland) Ltd, Electrofreeze (Equipments) Ltd, and the Soft Ice Cream Co Ltd all coming under its wing, as would subsequent Whippy companies.

Dominic soon turned his attention to the production of ice cream mix, as the pasteurised mix was being produced to the same recipe by companies in the Midlands, Hull and London. It was felt that Mr.Whippy should not be dependent on these outside suppliers and therefore should produce ice cream mix, in-house. To this end, negotiations to purchase their London supplier were entered into. On the 21st August 1961, Perfect Flavour Ice Cream Co Ltd became another Mr.Whippy acquisition, with MD and major shareholder Mr A E Pellosi remaining in day-to-day charge of the company.

Expansion during 1961 was in stark contrast to 1960 where all but six new Mr.Whippy vans were owned by franchise holders. Company operated depots began to emerge and (along with new franchise holders) Mr.Whippy was now close to being able to boast a truly national presence. By the end of 1961, 360 Mr.Whippy vans were on the road (all being Commer/Karriers), whilst several company depots were up and running (with more scheduled for 1962). From the outset they had enjoyed a strong presence in London and the Midlands, but with company depots such as Gateshead, Swansea, Welwyn Garden City, Tipton, Manchester and Paisley the Mr.Whippy brand was established as a truly national player, and one that the 'big boys' could no longer ignore.

To continue this rapid expansion through the latter part of 1961 and into 1962, Dominic negotiated to sell a 50% interest in Mr.Whippy (Softfreeze) Ltd, the owners of the Mr.Whippy franchise, to Northern Dairies Ltd. This was completed on 1st August 1961 and gave the Mr.Whippy group an important association with a publicly-quoted company.

By the end of 1961, Mr.Whippy had started to gain a greater momentum and confidence in the future! Therefore it felt assured of its role as a big player in mobiling. Electrofreeze in Southampton was turning out vans as fast as they could make them, as new franchise-holders were continuing to join the Mr.Whippy family and the growth of company-owned depots was continuing at a rapid pace. By the summer of 1962 there were 24 such depots and 48 franchise depots. That year was to be an extremely hectic one for Dominic and certain key personnel, notably Peter Hopkins and the group chief accountant, Roy Robertson. On the 13th January 1962 Mr.Whippy (Holdings) Ltd acquired from Dominic Facchino and Northern Dairies their shares in Mr.Whippy (Soft-freeze) Ltd, who were the owners of the Mr.Whippy franchise. Each party received 50,000 shares in Mr.Whippy (Holdings) Ltd.

Above: *By the end of 1962 there were 735 Mr.Whippy vans operating from 79 depots in England, Wales, Scotland and Northern Ireland. Pictured here is the (company-owned) Manchester depot circa 1962.* Photo Peter Hopkins

On the 31st January 1962 Dominic Facchino bought from Northern Dairies 24,000 shares in Mr.Whippy (Holdings) Ltd. This increased Dominic's personal holding in the company to 74 per cent, leaving Northern Dairies with the remaining 26 per cent.

Having purchased the Perfect Flavour company the previous year, the Group now undertook to build a 'state of the art' ice cream factory on a new two-acre site at Basildon in Essex. The factory cost £250,000 and had a production capacity of three million gallons of ice cream mix per annum. The new factory (run by A E Pelosi) was fully automated and came into production on the 1st July 1962. The plant also produced ice cream and ice lollies and boasted one of only two American built Vitaline production units to be installed in the UK. At this time a further six specially designed five- and seven-ton refrigerated vehicles were purchased to supply bulk loads to the growing Mr.Whippy depots.

Top Right: *After the successful pilot schemes in Birmingham and London in 1959, the Mr.Whippy brand became fully established ahead of the 1960 season. The vans were now in full livery with colourful 'point of sale' material. Adverts in the local press and some TV coverage helped Mr.Whippy quickly move from obscurity into national prominence.* Photo Peter Hopkins

Bottom Right: *Charles Forte regularly met with Dominic Facchino at London's Cafe Royal Sporting Club and these informal meetings led the two men to agree that Mr.Whippy would join the Forte Group. The amalgamation took place in October of 1962 and as a result made Dominic Facchino a millionaire. However, the continued financial success of Mr.Whippy under the Forte umbrella was not to last, and Charles Forte negotiated to merge Mr.Whippy with the Wall's mobiling operation.* Photo Peter Hopkins.

The rapid expansion of Mr.Whippy and the group's profitability led Dominic in the early part of 1962, to consider a public floatation. It was during these negotiations, that Dominic Facchino and Charles Forte used to meet at the Cafe Royal Sporting Club in London. Over their many informal chats about their respective companies, the topic of the floatation of Mr.Whippy arose.

Dominic had obviously whetted Mr Forte's appetite during these informal chats, and as a consequence it was decided to suspend any proposals for a floatation and enter into serious negotiations with the Forte Group. During the summer of 1962 an agreement was reached between the parties. It was agreed that Mr.Whippy (Holdings) Ltd would join, on amalgamation, with the Forte's (Holdings) Ltd floatation of the 11th October 1962.

Prior to these negotiations being completed by the two companies, Dominic had agreed to sell 23 per cent of his personal shareholdings in Mr.Whippy (Holdings) Ltd to Charles Forte. So at the point of amalgamation, Dominic Facchino held 51%, Northern Dairies 26% and Charles Forte 23%. At the Forte floatation, Dominic Facchino, Northern Dairies and Charles Forte sold their holdings in Mr.Whippy to the Forte group. The transaction being as follows:

> Dominic Facchino - 51,000 shares -
> consideration 1 million Forte shares
> Northern Dairies - 26,000 shares -
> consideration 350,000 Forte shares.
> Charles Forte (Nominees) - 23,000 shares -
> consideration 309,617 Forte shares.

With the value of Forte shares set at £1, this obviously made Dominic Facchino a very happy man, and of course, the newest member of the millionaire club. Not bad in just over three and a half years of operation. At the point of floatation there were 735 Mr.Whippy vans on the road, and from this number 374 were owned and operated from company depots. At this stage there were 23 company depots operated by various companies in the group and 56 depots run by franchised agents.

Top Left: *This rather poor quality photograph was taken in Middlesborough in the early 1960s, and clearly shows the American influence with use of bow ties and forage caps.* Photo Peter Hopkins

Centre Left: *Early Mr.Whippy vans had a 'Doppia' (drip feed) Carpigiani fitted as standard, with the later 1-ton vans using a 'Singola' (pump fed) machine. However, towards the end of the 30-cwt model's production run, a few vans were fitted with a brace of side-by-side single 'clock-face' machines.* Photo Unilever

Bottom Left: *Here is a survivor, which is still working in Queensland today. Back in the 1960s importing these vans from the UK was a costly affair due to transportation costs and the high Australian Import Taxes. With a UK cost of around £2,500, they were much dearer than the direct-drive Bedford CAs being produced by Cummins of Crewe. This cost meant that although Rootes continued to produce the BF chassis, Electrofreeze decided to move over to the Bedford CA in 1965.* Photo Trevor Thornton

I think it was fair to say that as 1962 came to a close, there was no doubt that Mr.Whippy ice cream could be bought in every densely populated area of England. Wales and Northern Ireland, with strong inroads being made through Mr. Whippy (Scotland) Ltd. This was also the year that saw the Whippy brand leave our shores for sunnier climes. However, this may never have happened, if it were not for a chance meeting (in a hotel bar) between Dominic Facchino and a Mr Bill Kendell, an ice cream operator from Sydney, on holiday in England.

On August Bank Holiday Monday 1962 a meeting took place between Dominic Facchino, key members of his staff and Mr Bill Kendell. Arising from this was an agreement to start a Mr.Whippy operation in Australia. Peter Hopkins who was present throughout, said, 'It was incredible to think that we had only one meeting with Bill Kendell. We were all very enthusiastic, we shook hands, drew up an agreement and simply went away and made it happen. If fact, we had ten Mr.Whippy vans on board a ship (at Southampton docks) bound for Sydney the very next month. Those were certainly exciting days'.

The Australian company (Mr.Whippy PTY Ltd) was formed with a capital of £35,001 (Australian pounds). Mr.Whippy (Holdings) Ltd. held technical control with 17,501 shares, while Bill Kendell, the new company's MD, held 17,500. The first batch of vans arrived at Sydney Docks and were unloaded on the 22nd of October 1962. These were all short-wheelbase models and were the first and last Commer/Karrier vans designed by Electrofreeze. This new design consisted of a forward-facing single Carpigiani machine located over the rear generator compartment. This new configuration afforded the operator better interior space and slightly less weight on the front axle. The first Mr.Whippy depot was at Rockdale with four of the ten vans working the streets of Sydney within four days of their arrival. Whilst negotiations with Forte were at their height during the summer of 1962, Dominic was invited to bid for a major share in another well known ice cream brand.

This company, called Treats Products of Leeds, was mainly involved in supplying the independent sector with a wide range of wrapped products. Ron Peters of Tonibell, already had an offer on the table to purchase 60 percent of Treats, and therefore Dominic needed to move quickly. However, Forte negotiations and other pressing matters precluded Dominic's personal involvement, so negotiations were entrusted to two key members of his staff. The outcome was successful with 80 percent of Treats being acquired by Mr.Whippy (Holdings) Ltd for a sum in the region of £180,000. However, this acquisition would have been quite sensitive at the time. For years independent mobilers had long been buying their products from Treats, and would not have been too happy about having to then buy their stock from the very people they were in competition with out on the streets. For this reason it is believed that special dispensation was given to leave this acquisition out of the Forte/Whippy prospectus. However, Mr.Whippy's holding in Treats was short-lived, and subsequently sold back to its former owners prior to Whippy's involvement with Wall's.

It was also a busy year for Dominic's brother Anthony, who had secured the contract to produce Mr.Whippy cones from his new factory (The Cake Cone Co.) in Tamworth Staffordshire in 1962. By the end of 1963, Anthony's company was boasting that it was 'one of the largest producers of cones in Great Britain - manufacturing at a steady rate of over 20 million cones a month!'. Whether or not this was exactly true, the company were certainly busy producing vast numbers of cones bearing the Mr.Whippy brand name. In fact, as demand rose, the company's order book soon became dependent on Mr.Whippy. As a consequence, full production capacity was soon turned over to Mr.Whippy, in order to meet the growing demand from the expanding network of company and franchise depots throughout the country.

Top Right: *Treat Products, the well-known Leeds firm, became part of the Mr.Whippy empire for a short period before being sold back to its former owners. The advert quotes a daily output of 30-tons of ice lollies every day and also shows a pair of the firm's bulk delivery lorries, which were refrigerated box vans on Bedford S-type 7-ton chassis.* Photo Ice Cream Alliance

Centre Right: *Although the Treat Products company was not a part of the Mr.Whippy (Holdings) portfolio for a very great length of time, it did cause concern for independent retailers who purchased their supplies from the Leeds-based business. One of the S-type delivery vehicles used by Treats is seen here prior to its delivery to Leeds in the 1950s. The un-dated picture is one of the few known views of any vehicle from this well-known ice cream company, so we make no excuse for using it here.* Photo Vauxhall Motors

Bottom Right: *The Facchino family business was famous for making cones and wafers. After the launch of Mr.Whippy, Anthony Facchino returned to what he knew best and formed 'The Cake Cone Company' in Tamworth. The biscuit delivery fleet used BMC FG box vans with the 'three-penny bit' cab.* Peter Hopkins

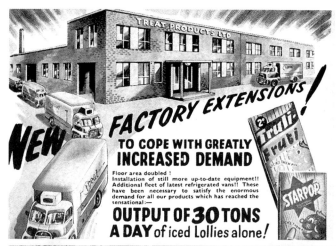

THE FORTE/WALL'S YEARS

As Mr.Whippy entered 1963 as an integral part of the Forte Empire, there seemed to be little day-to-day evidence of change. The Forte broom had obviously not felt the need to sweep clean and clearly demonstrated the faith that Charles Forte had put in Dominic Facchino and his team. Dominic therefore, remained as Chairman and Managing Director (with a lucrative 7-year contract), and Peter Hopkins continued as General Manager.

On paper the deal looked good, Mr.Whippy had demonstrated a healthy profitability in the previous two years, and Forte clearly believed that the best way forward was to keep a winning team at the helm. However this faith was not to be rewarded, as the financial success of Mr.Whippy was not to continue under the Forte umbrella. Charles Forte would soon learn that all was not rosy in the Whippy garden, as trading losses soon became evident. A source close to Charles Forte said, 'Charles felt rather let down by Dominic and his team. He clearly felt that they had taken their eye off the ball after the amalgamation. In fact he rued the day he got involved!'

Above: *After the amalgamation of the Mr.Whippy brand between Forte and Walls, opportunites of scale were presented to the company - one notable area was in central maintenance units, as seen here in the main Wall's workshops.* Unilever

In Charles Forte's biography, he clearly states this to be the case when looking back to his involvement with Mr.Whippy. 'Our accountants studied the figures and recommended the purchase. I was also impressed by the Chairman and Managing Director of the company. But I had made a mistake. As soon as I bought the company, the management seemed to lose a lot of interest and it was not long before Mr.Whippy was losing a lot of money'

In fact, losses would amount to £500,000, which in today's figures would be well over £5 million. Forte went on to say. 'It was a complete failure and in many ways a salutary experience. It proved to us that we were by no means infallible. It also taught me a lesson - never acquire a business however good it may appear to be, unless you are either guaranteed continuity of management, or you are in a position to replace the management'.

Top Right: *Forte were no strangers to the ice cream business as this picture demonstrates. Taken in 1958 the vehicle is a Vespa scooter: I'd probably guess it is a 125cc model, but I'm a Lambretta man myself!* Photo Ice Cream Alliance.

Centre Right: *Many independent mobilers and small fleet operators were converting hard vans to soft ice cream mobiles, and in most cases it was the Onan generator that made this possible. Weighing in at 375lbs, this LPG or Petrol fuelled (5kva) generator, meant that the popular Bedford CA could just about cope with the payload - but only just!*

Bottom Right: *Although poor in quality, this picture clearly illustrates the Mr.Whippy outlets that were to be found at Forte-operated motorway service stations.* Photo Peter Hopkins

It's not quite clear what Forte meant here by 'continuity of management,' as both managing director and general manager remained at the helm of Mr.Whippy throughout the Forte period and beyond. The situation in 1963 was clearly not helped by the recent imposition of purchase tax on ice cream and the worst winter the country had seen since 1947. However, to the general public, Mr.Whippy was a great success and fast becoming a household name. In spite of its losses the brand was set to embark on another phase of its life that spanned from the 1950s through into the 1990s and overseas into the 21st century.

The company may have been losing serious money, but to the drivers and franchise holders this was the heyday of soft ice cream mobiling, and sales by today's standards were extremely high. Michael Lloyd, whose father Peter ran the 20 strong Leamington Spa depot, said 'In those days it was not unusual to get through 30-gallons of mix a day. On one particular occasion, I can clearly remember pulling onto a housing estate and not having to move all day. Modern mobilers would find that extremely hard to believe, but it's true.'

During the summer of 1963 Charles Forte and Wall's started negotiations, as Wall's had clearly missed the boat with regard to their own involvement with soft ice cream mobiling and were keen to regain lost ground. Although Wall's were already running a limited number of soft ice cream vans, the company had failed to react to the early success and subsequent rapid growth of the Mister Softee and Mr.Whippy brands.

It would be fair to say that Wall's were not alone here in their sluggish response, because many others in the trade were in denial concerning the success (and therefore longevity) of soft ice cream mobiling during the early 1960s. Of the larger fleet operators, only Tonibell seemed to be making the wholesale transition to soft serve ice cream. Wall's therefore saw in Mr.Whippy, not only an opportunity to quickly catch up, but also the chance to eliminate a competitor in a market sector that they now needed to take more seriously. By the end of the summer of 1963, an agreement had been reached and a joint venture company would soon merge the Wall's mobiling operation with Mr.Whippy.

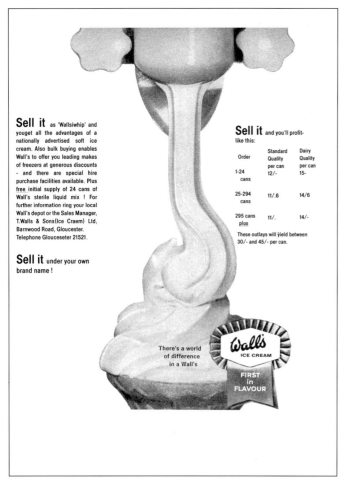

Sell it as 'Wallsiwhip' and you get all the advantages of a nationally advertised soft ice cream. Also bulk buying enables Wall's to offer you leading makes of freezers at generous discounts - and there are special hire purchase facilities available. Plus free initial supply of 24 cans of Wall's sterile liquid mix ! For further information ring your local Wall's depot or the Sales Manager, T.Walls & Sons (Ice Craem) Ltd, Barnwood Road, Gloucester. Telephone Gloucseter 21521.

Sell it under your own brand name !

Sell it and you'll profit-like this:

Order	Standard Quality per can	Dairy Quality per can
1-24 cans	12/-	15-
25-294 cans	11/.6	14/6
295 cans plus	11/.	14/-

These outlays will yield between 30/- and 45/- per can.

There's a world of difference in a Wall's

Wall's ICE CREAM FIRST in FLAVOUR

This arrangement would later be known as Walls-Whippy Ltd. and was to be a partnership of equals, with management and financial control jointly shared between Wall's and Forte. The number of directors would be increased from three to six to reflect the new structure, with three directors being appointed by Wall's and three from Forte. The official launch of this new joint venture was 1st of January 1964, although the company name was not changed until the 27th of January. The company (now renamed Walls-Whippy Ltd,) would continue to operate from the Mr.Whippy HQ at Warwick House, Leamington Spa.

Dominic Facchino remained as MD and Mr J Knowles (Wall's) was appointed Chairman, with Mr J Kinlock (Wall's direct selling) joining Peter Hopkins as Joint General Manager. The new joint venture company now boasted a mixed fleet of some 1,800 vans, with about 1,000 of these being soft serve. Walls had approximately 150 soft vans in their fleet, which were soon re-painted in Mr.Whippy livery at a cost of £30 per vehicle. Chimes were also changed to Greensleeves at a cost of £12 each. Wall's was now to supply tinned sterile mix to Walls-Whippy at an agreed transportation cost of 3d per tin. Wall's wrapped products would now be available on all Mr.Whippy vans, although this was rather restricted by the poor size of the freezer cabinet in the Commer/Karrier fleet.

In 1964, regular Mr.Whippy customers (with discerning palates) would have noticed a change in their ice cream, when the Mr.Whippy Ice Cream mix was replaced by Wall's canned sterile mix. The new Wall's canned mix (introduced in 1963) was called 'Wallsiwhip' and came in both Dairy and Standard form. The Mr.Whippy driver who came down our street at the time said that 'the customers much preferred the old recipe, but in no time at all everyone got used to the new flavour'. Changes at Mr.Whippy were not without their casualties, as Peter Hopkins recalls. 'We had a new 'state of the art' ice cream factory in Basildon, which would no longer be required, if Wall's joined with us. By late summer of 1963 the deal with Wall's was finalised in principal, and I knew what that would mean for our Basildon factory. Aturo Pelosi was our Chief Executive at the factory as well as a close friend. I had the unenviable task of travelling to Essex to break the news that his factory was to be closed and therefore he, and his staff, would be out of a job. That was tough!' The Basildon factory was eventually taken over by Rains Dairies Ltd.

Top Left: *When Wall's developed 'Wallsiwhip' in 1963, the writing was on the wall for Mr.Whippy's own 'mix production' facility in Essex. In 1964 after the formation of Wall's-Whippy Ltd, the standard quality canned 'Wallsiwhip' soon replaced the original Mr.Whippy recipe.* Photo Ice Cream Alliance

Bottom Left: *Although this picture is of a very poor quality, its inclusion in the book had to be considered because of the subject matter. This view clearly shows the re-branding of several MkI Bedford CAs from the Wall's fleet, following the coming together of Wall's Ice Cream and Mr.Whippy.* Photo Unilever

Above: *This interesting Unilever archive picture was taken just after the formation of Walls-Whippy in 1964, and shows a Wall's Morris LD repainted in Whippy colours. It has no soft-serve machine, but it boasts a new Golden Cornet introduced by Mr. Whippy and also shows a picture of scooped cones. In the absence of any other information it remains an interesting, but unanswered aspect of the Mr. Whippy story. However, it is fair to conclude that the product on offer must be Wall's soft scoop, which contrary to the slogan, was never introduced by Mr Whippy.* Photo Unilever Archive

Right: *Van number 3 is busy serving customers in front of Hotel Playa D'or on the Spanish Island of Mallorca. Introduced to the island in 1963, it's not known how long the Mr. Whippy brand lasted, or if any of the vans have survived today. These Mallorca vans were the same in every respect as the UK models, except for the slogans which were in Spanish.* Photo Peter Hopkins

Above: *By the mid 1990s, Wall's had effectively moved on from the Mr. Whippy brand. However, the traditional Mr. Whippy pink and cream livery refused to die, as many fleet operators selling Wall's products resisted the pressure to re-brand their vans in Wall's colours. Seen here is a 2000 model of a Whitby-Morrison built van, which in part helped the Whippy name continue into the 21st century. The van is part of the 'Donovan's Ice Cream' fleet based in East London, but it can be seen at events and shows all around the Home Counties.* Photo Andy Ballisat

Left: *The Cummins-bodied Bedford CF seen here with official Mr. Whippy transfers on a non-standard pink and white colour scheme was photographed in the late 1990s. The public's universal acceptance of the term 'Mr. Whippy' to describe a soft ice cream van, has led some other operators over the years to use, or should I say misuse, the brand name.* Photo Andy Ballisat

Above: *Pictured here is the author's 1961 Mr.Whippy van taken just prior to being retired from service in the 1990s by its then owner Mrs Barras. It is believed to be a Bonnalacks of Essex model and is built on a 30-cwt Commer 'BF' 3023 Chassis. It has a twin drip feed Carpigiani machine and the original 1703cc Ford powered TVO (12.5kva) generator. It is believed to be one of only three examples of this model to have survived down to today.* Photo Mrs Barass

Right: *Mr.Whippy vans made it into the movies on a few occasions. Notably in the opening and closing sequences of 'The Sandwich Board Man' (starring the comedian Michael Bentine) and the 1960s Beatles film 'Help'. Here, intrigued members of the public look on as a sequence in the Beatles film is shot in London's West End. Note the large cornet in place of the usual Mr.Whippy logos.* Photo courtesy of Walter Shenson

Above: *The taste of things to come! Not only is there a new image for Unilever Ice Cream Foods, but their mobiling also has a new shape, with the brand new Citroen Picasso vehicle complementing the more traditional ice cream vans. The Picasso will sell Cornetto Soft and impulse ice cream to consumers in places where larger vehicles are unable to go – a return to the ethos of the tricycles of 80 years ago.* Unilever

Left: *By way of contrast to the superb new mobiles that are being launched at the 2003 Ice Cream Alliance Exhibition in Blackpool (at the same time as this book), this colour view dates from the 1960s and shows part of the daily chores that a Mr.Whippy mobiler would have to do back then. This picture taken in the mid-1960s, shows some of the Mr Whippy fleet fuelling up at an Australian Esso garage. A plate on the generator's chassis stated 'Always use Esso Green TVO'. Esso garages also sold Mr.Whippy ice cream for a time.* Photo Peter Hopkins

WALL'S-WHIPPY LTD

It all sounded so simple, two leading brands with complimentary fleets, each having a national network of depots. Put them together to form Wall's-Whippy Ltd, what could be easier, 'a reasonably intelligent three year old could do it!' Wrong! First of all, no one was quite sure where all the vans were, then came the fact that the depots were either too large, too small, in the wrong place or even worse, didn't even exist. The majority of district and depot managers lived long distances from where they were needed, and to cap it all, Easter 1964 fell very early in the year, and ice cream sales were very poor. Many wished they hadn't entered into the joint venture....!

The objective was to integrate the (1,500 plus) combined fleet of hard and soft vans into both Wall's and Whippy depots at a ratio of somewhere in the region of 24 hard (wrapped) to 16 soft vans. The result would prove that a total re-think would have to be the order of the day. Chaos ensued and the new Head Office even struggled to provide basic services in many areas.

Above: *This Wall's Ice Cream Bedford CA, has a Smith's body in the livery of the early 1960s, and is fitted with a Carpigiani ice cream machine and Onan generator.* Photo Stuart Whitby

Existing Wall's managers were seconded to the new Wall's-Whippy depots to act on a number1/number 2 basis, but many who found themselves demoted to the number 2 position, predictably found other jobs. Several former Wall's personnel were also disaffected by what they saw as their 'New parentless status' and opted for self-employment under the Wall's-Whippy umbrella.

The next two years saw a great deal of change, and after the initial chaos, during and after the birth of Wall's-Whippy Ltd, a new optimism began to grow (albeit slowly) as the rationalisation and integration of the two fleets and depots became a workable reality. On the franchise front, new agents were continuing to join the brand in encouraging numbers. However, it soon became clear that the emphasis of Wall's-Whippy would have to move in the direction of a wholly franchised operation.

Top Left: *In the January of 1964, Wall's mobiling and Charles Forte's Mr.Whippy joined forces to form Wall's-Whippy Ltd. This was a partnership of equals that would continue until Wall's fully acquired the company in 1966. Some Wall's depots were excluded from the amalgamation, as were some of the older Wall's vans. Seen here are two of Wall's Trojan fleet of vans outside a Wall's depot in the early 1960s. Vans such as these were not included in the new joint venture.* Photo Unilever

Bottom Left: *In the troubled days after the formation of Walls-Whippy Ltd, it helped to keep a good sense of humour.* Photo Peter Hopkins

An entrepreneurial atmosphere was soon created as many ex-depot managers, senior personnel and selected van drivers were encouraged to take on a franchise operation. It's not clear exactly when Wall's-Whippy finances moved into the black, but the decision to move away from company owned depots and re-launch as a fully franchised operation was certainly a key factor in their future success.

At the end of 1963, prior to amalgamation, Wall's direct selling fleet consisted of 147 soft ice cream vans, 499 wrapped vans and 363 of the smaller 'minivans' such as the left hand drive Ford Thames 7cwt; of these, 611 operated under the new Wall's-Whippy company for the 1964 season. Some vans from the Wall's fleet, (such as the Trojans) were deemed to be too old to join the new combined fleet! Furthermore, some Wall's depots with a wholesale operation were also excluded from the new joint venture. Later, the full amalgamation of the Mr.Whippy and Wall's mobiling fleets would create an estimated 1,800 strong mixed fleet, and probably the largest in the country. Of these about 1,000 would be selling soft ice cream, branded in Mr.Whippy colours, whilst the remainder continued in the Wall's traditional blue & cream.

Whilst Mr.Whippy continued to make good profits for drivers and franchised depots, Wall's-Whippy Ltd as a whole was far less fortunate. By the end of the summer of 1964, a loss of £400,000 was recorded. The reason for this was stated as being due to the level of sales being 20% to 25% lower than anticipated. It was felt that the policy at this time should be directed towards break-even in 1965, although it was felt that this would not be fully achieved until 1966. Contributory factors for the failure to achieve planned sales were said to be: -

  a) The new company undertook too big a task in trying to operate over 1,500 vehicles.
  b) In general it was felt that the number of vans per depot had been too high.
  c) There had been a general recession in the mobiling industry.
  d) The rate of drivers 'fiddle' on soft ice cream had reached higher proportions than ever before.

The valuation of the mobiling fleet on the 1st of January 1965 was £1,400,000 (approximately £15 million in today's figures). This was felt to be far too high and was a direct consequence of a valuation method laid down in the heads of agreement between the two parent companies.

Clem's Cartoon

Parking Meters — Just what we wanted !

This tended to give an unrealistically high valuation to older vehicles and it remained a problem that would not be resolved until Wall's gained full control the following year. As previously stated, it soon became clear that Wall's-Whippy needed to reduce the number of company depots as well as reduce the number of vehicles per depot to no more than 24 vans. Wall's-Whippy Ltd, continued as a joint venture company for two years whilst struggling to get back into the black.

In 1966 negotiations between Wall's and Forte were concluded with Wall's purchasing Forte's interest, and therefore acquiring a 100 per cent share of Wall's-Whippy Ltd. However, Forte decided to retain its controlling interest in Mr.Whippy Australia. Although the Mr.Whippy saga left a bitter taste in Forte's mouth, the Forte Group's involvement with the Australian arm of Mr.Whippy must have proved more fruitful. They eventually sold Mr.Whippy Pty Ltd in December 1993.

Now fully under Wall's control, the Mr.Whippy brand would begin a new era. An era where company owned depots continued to decline in a gradual move towards a fully franchised network of depots running both Wall's and Whippy vans. By 1968 the whole Wall's-Whippy operation had become fully franchised and Wall's began to see positive results from their investment and restructuring programme. Anecdotal evidence suggests that in the better years that followed, the nationwide network of franchised dealers rose to around one hundred whilst the combined fleet numbers fell to around a thousand vehicles.

At one end of the scale were the small depots running 4 to 5 vans, whilst larger depots were operating a mixed (Wall's and Whippy) fleet of up to 30 vans. Franchise agents continued to join the Wall's-Whippy family with 150 new Morrison Electrofreeze CAs being purchased in 1968 alone. During this year, the 'Good Humor' mobile ice cream parlours were introduced on a trial basis, with nationwide coverage Dominic Facchino stayed at Wall's-Whippy for a short while, but his entrepreneurial spirit led him to pursue other business ventures.

Peter Hopkins also felt it time for a change and therefore decided to leave Wall's-Whippy. He subsequently joined Morrisons (Electrofreeze) Ltd in Southampton, where he stayed for many years. Much of this book could not have been written without Peter's fine memory and dedicated help over the past two years. Morrison's vehicle building division continued to supply Wall's-Whippy with vans until its acquisition by Robin Hood Engineering in the mid-1980s.

Top Right: *One of the 'baddies' mode of transport in the Beatles film 'Help' was a Mr.Whippy van. Here the driver waits for the high Priest (Leo McKearn) to return.* Photo Walter Shenson Pictures

Centre Right: *A rare, if rather poor picture of a prototype Mr.Whippy boat-style trailer designed for static operation. The trailer had its own generator and Carpigiani machine.* Photo Peter Hopkins

Bottom Right: *Walls-Whippy introduced the 'Good Humor' brand to British housing estates in the late-1960s as an attempt to compete with the Lyons shop based Napoli brand. It was not to be a great success!* Photo Peter Hopkins

An interesting footnote to the Mr.Whippy Story, is what happened to all those early Commer/Karrier vans when they were deemed to be uneconomical to keep on the road. A widely propagated rumour at the time, proffered the idea that Wall's rounded up all the Commers, loaded them onto a ship and then jettisoned them far out to sea. Nothing could be further from the truth, but the ice cream trade, is no different than others when it comes to rumours.

However, there is a story to be told, and one that was relayed to us by the now late Jim Smith, who used to work in Wall's fleet maintenance. Jim now takes up the story. ' In the late 1960s, a decision was made to start withdrawing from service some of the Commers in the Mr.Whippy fleet.

A decision was made to sell the vans at auction in Birmingham after the Mr.Whippy branding was removed, just leaving the pink and cream paint. This turned out not to be the best of ideas, as many of the vans came back into use as counterfeit Mr.Whippy vans using names (in our type-style) such as Mr.Woppy or Mr.Whirry; the lesson was learnt and no more vans were sold.'

'An enterprising dealer from South Wales called 'Jones' then negotiated a deal that would necessitate the vehicles being broken-up and the saleable parts exported. The vans were taken to a scrapyard at Sharpness Docks near Gloucester, which is probably where the 'dumped at sea' rumour originated.

The engines and generators were exported (by container) to Hong Kong, where it's believed that the engines went into junks and the TVO generators going over the border into China to generate an electrical power supply on communal farms. With other useable parts removed such as the Carpigiani machine, the vans were then scrapped.' This programme of scrapping the Walls-Whippy Commer fleet has meant that, the MTS, & Electrofreeze built vans have become extremely rare on our roads (and therefore the rally field), with only two known examples still working today. By comparison, the Mister Softee fleet reduced slowly in numbers over the years, and as a consequence a few more have survived the ravages of time.

Below: *Unfortunately, a detailed history of Mr.Whippy after Wall's fully acquired the brand in 1966, remains a mystery. After two years research, post-1966 archive material stubbornly refuses to surface, despite the help of the Birds Eye Wall's archives at Unilever. A detailed account of how the Mr.Whippy brand progressed after the Wall's acquisition will therefore have to be the subject of a future book in the 'Nostalgia Road' series. I therefore urge anyone with information, stories, anecdotes, pictures, documents and visual material to come forward. Of particular interest here is 'CHIMES' the house journal of Walls-Whippy Ltd, later to become simply the 'WALL'S JOURNAL'.*

Chimes

The House Journal of WALLS-WHIPPY LIMITED incorporating "THE DAILY SALE"

No. 1   SPRING   1964

WALLS-WHIPPY INTRODUCE NEW SALES WINNERS

LONG-RANGE WEATHER FORECASTS

TANGY FRUTIE   SUPER Z BAR   SNOFRUTE

THE BRAND IMAGE

Companies spend a lot of time and money developing their own distinct brand image and sometimes these are so successful that the brand itself slips into the background (and sometimes obscurity), while its brand name enters public consciousness to become a generic term for a whole group of products. In the case of soft ice cream, it would be quite unusual to hear someone say 'do you fancy a Rossi, or a Walls or a Nestles'.

The term Mr.Whippy has simply become a by-word for an ice cream served directly to the customer from a machine. In fact, only recently, at a local steam rally, I overheard a parent say, 'Johnny! Do you fancy a Mr.Whippy?' The two salient facts that clearly demonstrate this point were that the brand had been defunct for a decade and they were queuing at a Nestle' van.

Back in 1959 the Mr.Whippy product range was almost non-existent compared to today's wide range of wrapped lines. Vanilla ice cream, ice-lollies and family packs were all that was on offer, but the public nevertheless, lapped it up. By the 1960 summer season a fuller range of products were available, including Sundaes, Boats, and Dairy Flake cones, all backed up by full colour point-of-sale material for the vans' windows.

Above: *A selection of Mr.Whippy products from the early 1960s. Sundaes from 1/- ,Cones from 6d, Fruit & Banana boats 2/-, with fresh whipped cream in a "Strawberry Fayre" at 1/3d.* Photo Peter Hopkins

From the very start, Mr.Whippy realised the need for strong, forceful publicity to establish brand recognition. When a new area was opened up, large advertising space in the local press was taken out to announce the arrival of Mr.Whippy.

Company publicity at the time (1962) stated that establishing the brand was being achieved by 'the heavy use of national television coverage'; Mr.Whippy certainly made TV commercials, but heavy advertising on a national basis, is certainly debatable.

The slogan 'freshly made for you' really meant what it said when Mr.Whippy was launched back in 1959. Not only was the ice cream being made on the vans, the liquid ice cream mix was also being made fresh at the factory on a daily basis and transferred to bottles kept in the van's chiller compartment. However, as good a product as this was, it was not practical in terms of shelf-life and therefore distribution to an expanding fleet. When mix production moved to regional suppliers, mix would be supplied in polythene bags inside cardboard boxes.

Above: *Pictured here in 1963 is the Wall's Rotherham depot just prior to the formation of Wall's-Whippy Ltd. With the inescapable rationalisation that followed, depots such as this were either closed or expanded to accommodate Mr.Whippy vans.* Photo Unilever

This eventually gave way to sterilised mix in (US gallon) cans when Wall's introduced 'Wallsiwhip'. Canned sterilised mix was a fairly new technology developed by Lyons in the mid-1950s, but one that was not without initial problems. It wasn't just a simple case of putting fresh mix into a sealed can. The ultra high temperatures used in this process could (and did) adversely affect the taste. However, with taste difficulties resolved the can became de rigueur until tetra pack technology was introduced.

The first Mr.Whippy mix was formulated by L J Hynds at Meddocream in conjunction with Dominic Facchino. Tudor Dairies of Henley-in-Arden produced the fresh pasteurised mix for the Midlands and Mylo's of Chiswick did the same for the London area. As Mr.Whippy expanded, mix production went to York-Jones of Droitwich, Northern Dairies of Hull and Perfect Flavour Ice Cream Company of London; the latter was soon to come under the growing Mr.Whippy umbrella.

In 1959 the customer choice was severely limited, with only vanilla cones at 3d and 6d, and family packs and ice-lollies making up the range. However, this limited choice did not stop salesmen regularly achieving the sort of takings that today's mobilers can only dream of.

When franchise operations got fully underway by the 1960 season, the now familiar Mr.Whippy brand became fully formed. Sundaes and Banana Boats were introduced, with toppings from Margetts of Dalston, London. Ice cream cones at this time were supplied by Askeys of London, as Facchino Biscuits had ceased manufacturing ice cream cones and wafers.

In these early years, Mr.Whippy concentrated on the ice cream products that were freshly made on the vans, with wrapped products taking the back seat. Sundaes from 1/-, Banana Boats 2/- vanilla cones were now from 6d (six pence) with Dairy Flake and Sundae Cones costing 9d. A triple dairy treat called 'Strawberry Fayre' was also available at 1/3d. Some Mr.Whippy dealers were rather sceptical about the policy of promoting the more expensive lines 'as an adult confection in its own right'. However, by all accounts the sales figures showed that the more expensive lines did indeed exceed expectations.

In the very early 1960s, the sight of one of these pink and cream giants would have made quite an impact, on both children of the time and on established mobilers. 'Children's loyalties on my round crumbled when Mr.Whippy arrived' said one retired mobiler. In Coventry for example, the 30+ strong D Di Mascio fleet was a household name. So much so that most children referred to an ice cream as a 'D Di' The late Ugo Di Mascio was attributed as saying that 'only when Mr.Whippy came along did the Di Mascio stranglehold on children's affections get seriously damaged'. Up and down the country, as 'soft-ice franchise' operations expanded, a similar story was told.

By the mid 1960s the image of a standard Mr.Whippy van was certainly synonymous with the Rootes Group and its popular forward control Commer/Karrier chassis. I would imagine that for our older readers it is this image that has endured over the years! This is why we have chosen the Commer for our front cover, and not an Electrofreeze Bedford. Unlike the Smiths' built Mister Softee Commer, which changed little through its production run, MTS developed two variants, with Electrofreeze designing the final Commer chassised model. The original model (inherited from MTS of Feltham) was on a 30-cwt chassis with a rearward facing twin drip-fed machine. The second being on a 20-cwt chassis with a single (pump-fed) rearward-facing machine. From 1962 to 1965 the same 20-cwt chassis was employed with a more space efficient design with a rear-mounted forward-facing machine. All these models are now extremely rare with only a handful having survived the breaker's yard.

Like the shades of the paint on London's red buses and the green used by the top people's store, Harrods, Mr.Whippy was distinct in its own specific shade of pink and cream. The cream (British Standard Buttermilk) was easy to track down, but the pink was a completely different proposition. Personally having two early 1961 Mr.Whippy vans awaiting restoration, meant that tracking down the correct shade was an important factor in my research. Yet, at some point after Wall's acquired Mr.Whippy, they opted for a lighter shade of pink, with the older vans being repainted in the new shade. Not having any luck in the UK, an Australian friend managed to track down an original Queensland paint supplier to Mr.Whippy from the 1960s, who was still in business. More importantly, the company still had the early 1960s paint codes on file. At the time of going to press, a paint sample has arrived but the paint codes have yet to materialise.

Top Right: *In 1962 Bryan Whitby invented a direct drive system (taken from the van's engine to power the ice cream machine), making soft-serve vans much more affordable. But that's another story - see* Fifty Years of ice Cream Vehicles *by Alan Earnshaw & Stuart Whitby!*

Centre Right: *Management tried hard to get Coventry based D Di Mascio to join the Mr.Whippy franchise. The answer was no and Mister Di Di's was then established to compete on more even terms.*

Bottom Right: *The Morrison front-engined-drive diesel Transit.* Photo Andy Ballisat

MR. WHIPPY OVERSEAS

The concept of exporting the Mr. Whippy brand was probably not lost on the management team at the Leamington Spa head office. However, in the early days, establishing a strong national brand, through a network of company-owned and franchised operations was the obvious priority. This coupled with the need to ensure product and vehicle supply through partnership and acquisition, gave little time to consider exporting the Mr. Whippy brand. By contrast, the UK operators of the American Mister Softee brand, had, from the outset, envisaged a lucrative export market, particularly in countries where Lyons were already established. In 1959, Mister Softee (International) Ltd was incorporated and as a result quickly established several overseas operations. Dominic Facchino must have watched with great interest, and in the knowledge that there was a big market out there ready to be developed.

It must be remembered that Mr. Whippy (launched on a shoestring) did not have the advantage afforded to Mister Softee by their association with an international company of stature. However, by the summer of 1962 the scene was set for Mr. Whippy to be launched into what would become the largest mobile soft ice cream franchise outside of the United States and the UK at that time.

Above: *Mr. Whippy never made it to North Africa as this picture suggests. The photo was taken on a beach in Mallorca after a Mr. Whippy operation was set up on the Spanish holiday island in 1963. 'Try The New Ice Cream' became 'Pruebe el Nuevo Helado'.* Photo Peter Hopkins

Mr. Whippy Australia

After unusually brief but fruitful negotiations with Australian businessman, Bill Kendell, the first batch of ten Whippy vans left Southampton on the MV *Himalaya* bound for Sydney, Australia in September 1962. After many weeks at sea, the ship berthed on 22nd October in Sydney harbour, from where the vans were driven through Sydney to the first Mr. Whippy depot at Rockdale.

John Hiscott, (formerly depot manager Southampton), the new Sales Supervisor for Mr. Whippy Pty Ltd, recalls: 'There were some very uneasy moments for us, such as when it was thought that the doorways to the depot were not high enough to allow the vehicles through; and this only three days before their arrival. Also the time when it seemed that the drivers employed to operate the vans would have to take another test because the vehicles weighed more than 2-tons. This was not so bad, at least not until we were told that there was a four-week waiting list for driving tests in this category.'

A lot of problems had to be overcome, whilst engineer Sam Kingham (from Electrofreeze) worked round the clock, to get four vans on their rounds within four days and the following six a few days later.

The response by the Sydney public to 'new style' soft ice cream was to say the least, enthusiastic but Australia's largest city is spread over a very wide area and the Rockdale depot could not obviously cover the whole area, so in January 1963, a substantial new depot at Silverwater in the West of the city was opened to receive the bulk of the second batch of 24 vans. Within a few years, Mr.Whippy would expand into every State and in 1966 was listed on the Australian Stock Exchange, with Forte PLC maintaining the controlling interest. However, the dream was not to last, and in just a few short years the Mr.Whippy fleet started to fall into decline. In many areas there were continual problems with local authorities, and in some cases these councils were quite vociferous in their stance towards mobilers. This along with parental concerns over safety, and the enormous opposition from the business community, made life for some, very difficult indeed. But this was just part of the story, the cost of maintaining these large vehicles (to a high standard) was said to be far too expensive, and the impact of supermarkets and the rapid growth in home freezer ownership, was just another nail in the coffin.

The company therefore decided to cease operating a mobile fleet in favour of Mr.Whippy static sites. In 1968 the first Mr.Whippy Ice Cream parlour was opened and the last of the vans was said to have been sold off by 1970. Yet, anecdotal evidence indicates that this 'was actually completed at a later date. Bill Kendell at this time decided to resign and sell his interests in the company. In 1987 the company was de-listed from the Stock Exchange and became a wholly owned subsidiary of Forte PLC. In December 1993, after just over 30 years involvement with the Mr.Whippy brand, Forte sold out to Bonlac Foods Limited.

Today Mr.Whippy Pty Ltd is owned by South African born businessman, Mr Stan Gordon who is based in Melbourne. At present Mr.Whippy is only branded through a chain of thirty five static sites, which are primarily on the Eastern Seaboard of Australia. Today, the company are now looking at re-entering the mobile trade and are currently trialing one 'new-style' vehicle. So watch this space! Meanwhile, a few memories of the early days are now considered.

Top Right: *In 1962, Sam Kingham from Electrofreeze and John Hiscott depot manager, Southampton, (second and third from left) join their new Australian colleagues Pat McCabe, Jack McMurtie and John Garnham.* Photo Peter Hopkins

Centre Right: *An Electrofreeze MkIII Commer/Karrier. Note the front horizontal sliding window. MkI and MkII models had the better vertical (counter-balanced) windows.* Photo Peter Hopkins

Bottom Right: *At the time of writing Mr.Whippy Australia currently has this new mobile sales van under trial, where the driver serves from outside the vehicle.* Photo Stan Gordon.

Top Left: *We see here a rather radical departure from the traditional Mr.Whippy Man logo. In an age of electronic chimes, the old mobiler's hand bell does seem rather odd, if not a pleasing choice.* Photo Stan Gordon

Bottom Left: *With the introduction of the MK3 version, the Mr.Whippy Commer gained valuable interior space. The Carpigiani was moved from its forward position and located in previously wasted space where the upper generator compartment had been. The water tap was also moved from the counter top, therefore allowing more space for cones, wafers and Sundae equipment.*

Bob Staff, now of Hervey Bay, Queensland, but then a resident in Victoria recalls how he got involved with Mr.Whippy in Australia, saying:- 'It all started one fine day in the middle of winter whilst standing in a cargo shed at Victoria Dock, West Melbourne in or about June 1965. I was waiting for my shift to start, when my eyes focussed on three shiny pink and cream, brand spanking new Mr Whippy Commer vans, just unloaded from a ship's hold. I thought that they were the most beautiful vehicles that I had ever seen and was hoping that when I boarded the ship, I would get the chance to help discharge more of these vans, presumably just arrived from the U.K. Little did I know at this time what a huge part that these vans would play in my life.

It was to be a great life as a Mr Whippy man, because you were regarded almost as a national hero as the company took on the Local Authorities. There were some significant legal victories and these forced changes to some laws so the general public loved us, but the business community hated us. I had the fortune or misfortune to be the first Ice Cream Van to sell in Victoria's busiest holiday area during the annual summer holiday period, what a baptism of fire that was!

The first couple of hours went really well, then, as I started vending along a section of foreshore very close to the beach, I was confronted by a vigilante group of shopkeepers armed with buckets who insisted on dashing down to the sea filling their buckets with sea water and hurling it in the window every time I opened it, what a mess. The next day my boss sent a big tough looking trainee with me to ride shotgun I also armed myself with a solid wheel brace extension and off we went, back down to the seaside. My trainee got cold feet just before we started selling, abandoned ship (van) and deserted me. Ah well, I'm here now I might as well push on. Almost straight away they turned up again and started urging my customers to come over to their shops, a customer said to their ringleader "stand aside and let my kid buy his Ice cream" with that, the ringleader hit him and knocked him to the ground.

Quickly on the scene, the police charged the ringleader, confiscated my wheel brace and ordered me to leave town or else be locked up. I rang my boss, he rang the police, and they told him, if I didn't leave, he had better jump in his car and bring plenty of bail money with him. As our solicitors could not be contacted, I had to retreat. Eventually I was called as a witness in the assault case but the shopkeeper was let off because of his previous good record as a policeman in the police service.'

In 2002 Bob's son Robby decided to play detective, in an effort to see if his father's old van (No. 24) had survived the ravages of time. His efforts eventually paid off as it was found in a complete and driveable condition. After much haggling, a price was negotiated and a deal struck! However, the van was some 3,000km away from home and to trailer the van back was not only very costly, but also meant entrusting his valuable cargo with unknown operatives. The decision was therefore taken to drive this nearly 40-year old van back from Melbourne. This was quite a brave (or foolhardy) undertaking, and one that would take about five days or so to complete; but with Robby's car packed with every spare part he could cram in with his tools, the convoy slowly made its way safely to its new home at Hervey Bay.

Mr Whippy New Zealand

Early in June 1964 a decision was made to break into the New Zealand market on a totally franchised basis with one or more agents. General Foods Ltd, the dominant ice cream supplier in New Zealand at the time, had agreed to take on the Mr.Whippy franchise, with an expected 24 vans to be shipped ready for their 1964 summer season. Again the public's acceptance of Mr.Whippy in New Zealand was enthusiastic, and van numbers grew close to an estimated 50 vehicles at its peak. The Kiwi version of Mr.Whippy is now in its 40th year and boasts that it is New Zealand's 'most renowned soft serve ice-cream retailer' as well as a Kiwi 'National Icon'.

Although the brand has not enjoyed continuity of ownership over the years, it has however survived, and now remains the only official Mr.Whippy brand being marketed via a mobile fleet today. Formerly owned by NZMP Ltd, (the domestic arm of the giant dairy company Fonterra Co-operative Group), the current owners are Mr.Whippy New Zealand Ltd. They claim that 'Mr.Whippy is one of New Zealand's oldest and most renowned franchise systems with brand awareness reaching 97% amongst all New Zealanders'.

The 1989 owners, Taylor Freeze, restructured Mr.Whippy as a formal franchised system based on exclusive territories. Today, the level of mobiles on the road is less than at its peak, with thirty six vans operating through the same number of franchises. In 2003 Mr.Whippy's new owners have embarked on an expansion plan, with five new Mr.Whippy mobiles recently on the road.

Top Right: *Discovered in 2002, this van is pictured when new on page 20 (top) and is now being restored from the chassis up by owner Robby Staff, who lives in Hervey Bay Queensland.* Photo Robby Staf

Centre Right: *'Enjoy a sundae today!' proclaims the advert at a cost of 1/6d in Australian shillings. This young customer looks as if he is about to enjoy one of the more expensive Sundae boats at 2/-, kids on my round had to settle for 6d cornets.* Photo Peter Hopkins

Bottom Right: *An Australian Mr.Whippy parlour in the 1990s showing the Mr.Whippy 'Running' Man logo and two Taylor Freeze machines.* Photo Robby Staff

Top Left: *Upwards of 200 Electrofreeze-built vans were exported to Australia, Tasmania and New Zealand in the mid-1960s. These vans were built to the same specification as UK models except for additional vents set into the front panel under the headlights.* Photo Peter Hopkins

Centre Left: *This Karrier-badged MkIII van is pictured at the seafront on the Spanish holiday island of Mallorca in 1963. The Commer/Karrier range had the Humber Hawk petrol engine with optional porous chrome bores as an aid to 'stop-start' driving.* Photo Peter Hopkins

Bottom Left: *The introduction of Mr.Whippy to Mallorca was, by all accounts, well received. The introduction of a right-hand-side sliding window in 1962 also enabled the driver to serve onto Spanish pavements.* Photo Peter Hopkins

Mr.Whippy Spain

Also at this time, a Mr.Whippy operation was started on the Spanish holiday island of Mallorca. Based in Palma, the operation was in partnership with Marisa of Barcelona, the company being called Mr.Whippy (Espana) Ltd. So on the 6th of June (D-Day) 1963, the first consignment of vans in shiny new Spanish livery left the Electrofreeze factory in Southampton bound for Mallorca.

'Try the New Ice Cream' became 'Pruebe el Nuevo Helado' and 'Freshly made for you' became 'Recien Hecho Para Ud!' The convoy of Mr.Whippy vans travelled overland (via Dunkirk) to Barcelona and then on to Palma de Mallorca by ferry. The French and Spanish public hadn't seen anything like a Mr.Whippy van before, and therefore the vans attracted a great deal of attention wherever they went.

After a few days of cleaning, checks and driver-training, Mr.Whippy was ready to undergo a trial run out on the rounds. The 'Nuevo' ice cream was dispensed free on this occasion and as can be imagined, went down very well indeed. The ice cream mix was made to the Mr.Whippy formula by the Marisa Ice Cream factory, under the watchful eye of Mr Pelosi who was running the Mr.Whippy factory at Basildon.

Meanwhile, a civic reception by the Mayor of Palma was arranged to officially welcome Mr.Whippy to the island. This event was held after a convoy of polished vans paraded through the centre of Palma. In attendance was the British Consul and the Chief of Police, along with Mr J Morrell (Mr.Whippy Espana) and Mr Arturo Pelosi (Mr.Whippy UK). After the reception, the Mayor, Chief of Police and dignitaries inspected the vans and tried the exciting new ice cream with many exclamations of 'Muy bien'

For whatever reason, Mr.Whippy did not develop any new export markets after this hectic but brief two-year period. This does seem rather strange, as both Forte and Wall's had a strong international dimension to their operations. Nevertheless, despite failing to match the Mister Softee export success, Mr.Whippy exported upwards of 200 vehicles to Australia and New Zealand and in doing so, developed their operation into a brand leader in both countries.

Mr.Whippy Ireland

Closer to home, Mr.Whippy travelled across the Irish Sea to Dublin. Little has been uncovered about this operation, which was started in June of 1963. This operation was in partnership with a Mr Brendan Bradley of Lucan Dairies.

The company operated under Mr.Whippy (Ireland) Ltd and ran 12 vans. If any readers can throw more light on the operation of Mr.Whippy vehicles in Ireland please contact me via Trans-Pennine Publishing, PO Box 10, Appleby CA16 6FA.

Mr.Whippy USA...?

Mr.Whippy was never exported to the United States, officially that is! However, the Mr.Whippy man with his Tudor bonnet and dancing feet appears to have become the registered logo for Mister Whippy of Chincoteague Island in the state of Virginia. The story goes that a man named Lee Savage and his wife Wilma, opened an ice cream shop in the 1950s called 'Dari Dream' but later changed the name to Mister Whippy and adopted the official Mr.Whippy logo.

In the early 1970s they imported about a dozen Morrison-built ice cream vans from the UK, which ran under the Mister Whippy brand. These were in the yellow and white livery that was then employed on this Virginian island. In the late 1980s the owner Mr Savage retired, closed the business and all but three of the vans were sold off.

In the summer of 1991, the Conklin family of Chincoteague re-opened the business, which is understood to have been previously operating under a different name. The Conklins decided to rename the ice cream business Mister Whippy in order to match the name on the remaining vans. The business grew considerably and in 1997 Mister Whippy moved to its present location on Maddox Boulevard in Chincoteague and in 2001 a new van was purchased to continue with mobile sales.

Top Right: *On warm summer days Mister Whippy himself makes an appearance at this American ice cream parlour. Mind you, I think our Mister Whippy seen here has put on a few pounds and where are those 'dancing' feet?* Photo Richard Conklin

Centre Right: *Although appearing to be a Bedford CA, this Morrison built 'Powerdrive' van was actually one of several of the kind imported to the State of Virginia in the early 1970's. It is built on a unique chassis which is believed to be the only chassis ever commissioned by an ice cream coachbuilder. The vehicle employs a power take-off from the vehicles gearbox which in turn operated a 12kva alternator to power a triple head Carpigiani.* Photo Richard Conklin

Bottom Right: *In 2001, British-style coach-building returned to Chincoteague Island, USA, in the form of a new Whitby-Cummins van, or should I say truck. Note the American spelling of Mister Whippy as opposed to that seen elsewhere. On the door is our old friend with the 'dancing feet', now a registered US trade mark.* Photo Richard Conklin

THE VEHICLES

Although the early Mr.Whippy vehicles are clearly associated with the Commer/Karrier BF model, this was not the only chassis to be employed for soft ice cream vans in the fleet over the years. It is therefore important to look at the four main choices, on a maker-by-maker basis.

COMMER/KARRIER

The Commer/Karrier 'BF' model was the preferred choice of both Mister Softee and Mr.Whippy back in 1959 and remained so for around six years . The 'BF' model started life as the 'AF' in the early 1950s and had evolved from the post-war Q25 model, which was effectively a pre-war design that remained in production for several years after its successor's launch. The 'A' and 'B' designation referred to the production series and the 'F' indicated that it was forward control. The first of these new Commers were 25-cwt models with a gross permissible laden weight of 65-cwt and powered by a 2266cc side valve engine carried over from the Q25.

Above: *The BF Commer started life as the AF model in the 1950s, here the prototype MkIV chassis cowl model is seen in May 1953. The BF continued in production post 1965, although Electrofreeze stopped using this popular Rootes chassis that year.* Rootes Official

In late 1953 the model was updated to the Mk IV and designated AF2523. Later in 1957, the sturdy side-valve engine was replaced with the overhead valve unit from the Humber Hawk, which yielded an additional 6bhp. The gross vehicle weight was also increased to 72cwt and designated BF3023. The 30 stood for 30-cwt and the 23 was the last two digits of its 123 inch wheelbase. In 1959 a short-wheel-base (1-ton) version was introduced with a 12" shorter wheelbase, a one piece propshaft and slightly higher back axle ratio, which gave a modest increase in top speed. This version was designated BF2011 and was the only chassis used (albeit extended) for the whole production run of Mister Softee Commers. The standard BF 1-ton chassis was probably adopted by Mr.Whippy in early 1961 and totally replaced the longer 3023 chassis by the later part of 1962.

Top Right: *The Commer's origins were essentially a reworked Q25 chassis from the 1940s. Here we see the new 25-cwt version on show in Hotpoint livery at the Commercial Motor Show.* Rootes Official

Centre Right: *The ubiquitous Bedford CA appeared in many guises from 1952 onwards, and was very obvious from its split-screen windscreen and short, stub-like (piggy) nose. It became a real favourite in chassis cowl form, and was supplied to a variety of bodybuilders for a variety of applications. Here we see one of the very first chassis cowls to be produced, carrying a crew-cab body by Spurling.* Vauxhall Motors

Bottom Right: *Again another first, this time the very first Bedford CF, which rolled off the Dunstable production line in panel van form in August 1969. It was the doyen of a model range that still remains popular with mobilers today.* Vauxhall Motors

THE UBIQUITIOUS CA/CF BEDFORDS

Long before Mr.Whippy was launched in the late-1950s, the CA Bedford had become a favourite of the 'mobiling' trade in the early-1950s and today is still held in great affection by many. To help keep these CA and CF models running, companies such as Adrian Bailey Classics of Batley, West Yorkshire provide a useful service by supplying both advice and spare parts.

Launched in 1952 the CA had all the qualities that made it ideal for a coachbuilt ice cream van, added to which it was cheap to buy, cheap to operate and cheap to maintain. The normal semi-forward control van had a split windscreen, a separate 90-inch wheelbase chassis and boasted two front sliding doors (slam-doors were available on chassis cowl models, which were common on most ice cream vans). The early models obviously did not have the carrying capacity of the later 15- to 17-cwt models, but above all, they were comfortable and easy to drive.

The CA started life with a 10- to 12cwt chassis and boasted independent coil front suspension and access to the engine bay from inside the vehicle. This was done without compromising interior space and the column-mounted gear lever was a boon for the mobiling trade. With a 1507cc petrol engine from the Vauxhall Wyvern, the CA cost (in chassis cowl form) £438 inc. purchase tax. A Perkins diesel was offered in 1961, but after several facelifts and a 17-year production run, the CA bowed out in 1969.

With the launch of the Ford Transit, Bedford could no longer sit on its laurels and do nothing, so they turned their eyes to the United States for a solution; the result was a scaled down version of a General Motors panel van. Designated the CF it was launched in 1970 and available in short and long wheelbase models, and built in five chassis weights, right up to a twin wheeled 35-cwt model.

The mobiling trade took to the CF in the same way as it did the CA, and today many CF's are still working hard for their owners. The model competed well against the Transit and remained in production until 1987.

Top Left: *By the 1980s, the Ford Transit had certainly become the mobiler's preferred choice. Here in traditional Mr.Whippy pink and cream is a 1989 Transit with Whitby-Morrison long cowl bodywork.* Photo Stuart Whitby

Centre Left: *Here with its bulbous front end is a MK1 Diesel Transit in Mister Softee colours. With Bedford still being the preferred choice back in the 1970s, only a few early Transits were ever bodied for Mr.Whippy.*

Bottom Left: *End of the line! They say every picture tells a story and this picture is no exception. In the early 1960s these vans would have cost more than a large detached house, but in the late 1990s, they were just scrap value. However, two vans from this small fleet (off camera) have survived and are now in preservation.* Photo Joan Barras

THE FORD TRANSIT

Prior to 1965 Ford had its Ford Thames 400E range, but although these were available in chassis cab form, they were not as widely used by specialist builders (eg ice-cream mobiles) as the Bedford CA models were. To Ford this was posing a serious problem, and in the summer of 1961 a decision was taken to create a new pan-European delivery van. Ed Baumgartner, an American product planner was given the task of creating this van, and he arrived in England in the autumn of 1961.

From the outset he knew that there were insufficient funds to build a completely new, fully rationalised vehicle, and that many of the larger costlier components would have to be acquired from existing product linesl. The Transit was thus born from a marriage between two unlikely parents, the Thames 400E from Dagenham and the German FK (Ford Koln)Taunus. Both of these models had experienced a poor sales record and they needed replacing.

Although the Ford Transit did not initially become the preferred vehicle platform for Mr.Whippy after its launch, it did become very popular in later years, right through to the demise of the Whippy brand. It's now hard to believe that the Mk 1 Transit was launched way back in 1965, but it must have given Bedford quite a fright with their ageing CA model, which had to battle on until the CF became available four years later.

The Transit was marketed as the van that drove with the comfort of a car whilst being rugged enough to cope with heavier payloads. The narrow V4 petrol engine allowed a semi forward control layout with no engine intrusion into the cab. An all-new engine was developed for the Transit, but was initially fitted into the Ford Corsair; fitting a car engine into a van was far more acceptable than the other way round. A Perkins 4108 engine with its bulbous front end came next with the face-lifted Mk II to take the Transit into the 1970s. Then Ford fitted their in-line four cylinder crossflow petrol engine along with a Ford-built diesel. Today the Transit has moved to front wheel drive and remains the UK mobiler's number one choice.

THE PIED PIPER

To the detriment of many a mother's purse, the ice cream man's chime has often had the same effect on children as did the tune played by the 'Pied Piper of Hamlin'. It is therefore no mistake that the name of the chimes used on Mr.Whippy vans was the Harvin 'Pied Piper'. Mister Softee and Tonibell had decided to commission their own distinctive tune, as Wall's had also done with their 'Stop Me And Buy One' tune earlier in the 1950s. Dominic Facchino decided to use that most English of tunes,' Greensleeves' , allegedly written by Henry VIII. Dominic must have been quite inspired by our King Henry, as the smiling face of the Mr.Whippy man also wears a Henry VIII Tudor style bonnet. However, it is understood that the main reason was due to the fact that the Greensleeves tune was royalty free.

Ron Peters of Tonibell is the man accredited with the idea of replacing the mobiler's hand bell with an amplified musical chime. In 1954 he approached Harvin with a large American chime unit which employed tuned metal bars struck by hammers. He asked them if they could produce a smaller, cheaper and more reliable unit, which they did. Harvin took a Swiss musical box movement and attached a magnetic pick-up, which fed the sound to a speaker horn, via a valve type amplifier.

Although the resulting sound was good, this arrangement was rather heavy, and like the power hungry, valve-operated car radios of the period, tended to drain the battery. By the time Mr.Whippy and Mister Softee were launched in the spring of 1959, the transistor was a reality and had already been utilised by Harvin to produce the now ubiquitious Pied Piper chime.

Above: *No mention of the Mr.Whippy vehicles would be complete without reference to the chimes they carried. The sheet music above is Greensleeves, which was Mr.Whippy's 'call-sign' from its launch in 1959 and is still used today as a registered trademark by Mr.Whippy New Zealand.*

Although technology has moved on with electronic chimes, many mobilers still favour the mechanical Pied Piper unit, which must be said, has given sterling service over many decades and, to Harvin's credit, with little need for change.

In the 1960s the sound of 'Greensleeves' would certainly have meant that Mr.Whippy was in your neighbourhood. This would have equally applied to Tonibell, Wall's and Mister Softee with their unique and distinctive chimes. However, as these famous brands faded away (except Wall's), their chimes began to be adopted by many independent mobilers up and down the country. Today, and for those old enough to remember, these chimes are a regular reminder of those famous brands and the golden era of mobiling, now sadly, long gone.

Right: *Dominic Facchino gave Mr.Whippy a Henry VIII style bonnet and 'dancing feet'. It's therefore no coincidence that Mr.Whippy danced to the Tudor tune, Greensleeves.* Photo Jean Yates.

TRACTOR VAPORISING OIL

It may seem strange to have a chapter in this book with a heading relating to agricultural equipment, but for at least the first decade or so, tractor fuel (then commonly available) was an integral part of the daily Mr.Whippy operation. It will be recalled that when Mr.Whippy was launched back in 1959, the company chose the Rootes group Commer/Karrier 'BF' 30 cwt chassis as a platform for their new 'factories on wheels'.

This choice of a larger size chassis was made necessary, due to the weight penalty inflicted by the twin Carpigiani ice cream machine and the heavy 12.5kva, TVO fuelled generator sets. But what is TVO? Long since withdrawn from general supply, Tractor Vaporising Oil' is now only sold by a few local suppliers. These companies blend readily available ingredients to various recipes as a replacement for this now defunct fuel. But years ago TVO was manufactured by most of the major oil refiners?

Part of a family of burning oils which includes paraffin, diesel and the twenty eight second oil used in domestic central heating boilers, TVO is a middle distillate premier grade burning oil (kerosene) with an improved aromatic content.

Above: *Soft ice cream was once dominated by vans with TVO generators, such as this three-phase 12.5kva generating set, which was the largest to be used at that time.* Photo Unilever

Standard grade kerosene is obtained from crude oil as a fraction with a boiling range of about 150/250 degrees centigrade. Because it did not attract a high duty as petrol did, kerosene had become established a long time ago as an engine fuel. It was generally used in spark ignition engines with exhaust/inlet manifold heat exchangers, to vaporise the fuel and having low compression ratios to suit the low octane number of about 15/20.

'Paraffinic crudes' were most suitable for wick-type burners in lamps and heaters because of their low tendency to smoke, but rather poor as engine fuel due to a lower octane number. Conversely, napthenic and especially aromatic crudes had lower burning and smoke qualities, but were better engine fuels as they had a higher octane number. Premier grade burning oil was developed from the standard grade by using extraction processes to remove a large proportion of the aromatic content. Although the burning quality improved, the engine performance deteriorated as the octane number fell towards zero.

Tractor vaporising oil came into being as an improved kerosene for engine applications by blending into the kerosene, the higher octane aromatics which had been stripped out to produce a premium grade burning oil. By this means, TVO acquired an octane number in the order of 55/70. From the point of view of distillation characteristics and ease of vaporising in the inlet manifold, there is nothing to choose between TVO and standard grade kerosene. However, the octane quality of the latter is rather poor and will, in almost, all cases produce engine knock.

Having spoken to many TVO tractor enthusiasts over the years, it became apparent that there are many home made blends of TVO, in fact too many to list here. However, the general consensus is that a preferred measure of petrol is added to kerosene (to lift the octane rating) along with an upper cylinder lubricant. All the different blends work, it's simply which works best in your engine.

Aztec Oils Ltd of Bolsover, are one of the few companies that still blend TVO in small quantities. Their formula is as follows:-

75% kerosene + 18% petrol + 8% ISO 32 mineral oil.

Due to major changes in tractor engine manufacture Shell finally withdrew their 'Shellspark' TVO in 1974, but as many 'older' engines were still in use, they were obviously asked for a replacement formula. Shell suggested at the time that petrol was added to Kerosene in 10% increments (up to a maximum of 50%) until engine knock disappeared. Ron Knight, a well-respected TVO tractor enthusiast, is typical of the breed and swears by his own formula: - 70% kerosene + 20% petrol + 10% diesel.

When TVO became scarce in the latter half of the 1970s, some operators felt forced to use straight petrol to run their generators. This proved unsatisfactory and not just on the grounds of cost. Industrial (low compression) spark ignition engines were not designed to run on modern petrol. This would have resulted in some loss of power, but more importantly the inefficient burning of the fuel would have caused the engine to run hotter than when TVO fuel was used. Replacing the head gasket to increase the compression ratio was one way to improve matters, but along with other factors, it was not long before the Commer/Karrier ice cream van with its TVO generator, became a rare sight and smell!

Top Right: *This AC Morrison 12.5 kva generator set uses an industrial version of Ford's 1703cc Consul engine. It starts on petrol and is then switched over to TVO when warm.* Photo Ice Cream Alliance

Centre Right: *Reciprocal trading? Mr.Whippy ice cream could be bought at selected Esso garages, whilst a plate on the generator's sub-chassis stated, 'Always use Esso TVO'.* Photo Peter Hopkins

Bottom Right: *When Wall's sold off their older vans some of them began to reappear as the opposition. Wall's therefore made the decision to scrap all further redundant vans rather than sending them to auction.* Photo Mark Sykes

THE OPPOSITION

At the beginning of 1959 when plans to launch both Mr. Whippy and Mister Softee were coming to fruition, the number of national ice cream brands could be counted on one hand, these were notably Wall's, Lyons Maid, Eldorado and Neilsons, all of whom ran (hard ice cream) mobile fleets. These brands, like independent mobilers, were all affected when they came head-to-head with the 'New Style' ice cream from the men in their large American inspired 'factories on wheels'. But who was Mr. Whippy's true opposition? Very early in the 1960s, it would be true to say that on a national level, only Mister Softee was comparable and therefore Mr. Whippy's only true opposition. In reality this was far from the case, as competition was different from area to area and region to region.

Above: *Although hard ice cream sales were seriously affected in those areas where soft ice cream rounds were established, everyone still made a good living. In fact it is a good time to point out that mobile sales of freshly made soft ice cream was in fact available long before the advent of Mister Softee or Mr. Whippy, as the only thing that was really 'new' was the idea of making it on the van rather than a few hours earlier, which was normally the case with the small quality manufacturer.*

Old mobilers will often argue about who first introduced 'Soft Ice Cream' to our streets, but it was in fact Mister Softee by about a month. Yet, market penetration didn't happen overnight and some areas did not see either brand for a few years, by which time other operators were getting in on the soft ice cream act.

Top Right: *Criterion Ices of Sydenham sold superb Gold Medal 'soft scoop' ice cream on my South London round and the public loved it! Companies such as Mr.Whippy therefore, did not always have it all their own way.* Photo Ice Cream Alliance

Centre Right: *In 1961 Mr.Whippy's factory manager, Mr A E Pelosi, was also the MD of the newly launched Mr.Tasty ice cream brand based in Plaistow, East London. The vans were built by Bonallack & Sons Ltd of Basildon in Essex and were in nearly all respects, the same as the Electrofreeze models.* Photo Ice Cream Alliance

Bottom Right: *This MTS bodied Gallone's van is the last known survivor from the West London coachbuilder. It regularly works Northampton market.*

In densely populated South London where I worked in the 1960s, the competition was strong, with Whippy, Softee, Tonibell and a host of independents vying for trade. On many occasions over those years several vans would be at the same stop, park or show together. The interesting thing was that the soft vans did not always have it all their own way, for instance Criterion Ices produced a superb award winning ice cream that the public loved. On many occasions I witnessed a longer queue at the Criterion van than at the competitors, and when I bought my own soft van, I soon learnt to steer clear of Criterion's times.

The public lapped up the idea that 'Freshly made just for you' produced a better ice cream, compared to a product made just a few hours earlier. Long before soft scoop was invented, drivers such as myself would take freshly made soft ice cream straight from open vertical batch freezers out onto our rounds. We scooped or spooned the ice cream, which due to lack of high overrun, had a pleasing consistency different from most of today's ice cream. Ice cream made this way plays no part in today's commercial production of ice cream, but is, to my mind, still the connoisseur's choice.

Mr.Whippy and Mister Softee had a fairly easy time of it for a season or two after their launch, but the regional fleets and individual mobilers were soon busy converting vans to soft ice cream, or buying new from the several companies offering soft-serve vans. By competing on more even terms, the local brands would fare much better and in many cases would out-sell the big boys. There were of course some organisations such as Curli Top and Mr Tasty who planned to develop fully into a national brand and therefore compete head-on with Mr.Whippy.

Of these Mr Tasty is worth a particular mention here, if only due to the fact that its 'supremo' was Mr A E Pelosi of the Perfect Flavour Co. This London firm made ice cream mix for Mr.Whippy and it seems rather strange that Dominic Facchino, allowed his factory manager to launch a soft ice cream brand that could eventually pose a commercial threat to Mr.Whippy. Conceived in the early part of 1961 Mr Tasty (Italian Maid) Ltd was (with its four directors) reported to have quickly opened four depots in London and The Home Counties. The vans were nearly identical to the 30-cwt Mr.Whippy Commers, except the fact that they were built by Bonallack & Sons Ltd of Basildon in Essex.

1920s

1930s

1940s

1950s

Wall's has been the outright owner of Mr.Whippy since 1966, so it is appropriate to take a look at this most famous of brand names in this volume. Wall's can trace its origins back to the late 18th Century, when the young Richard Wall was an apprentice in what is now London's fashionable West End, working in a meat and pie business at St James' Market. In 1806 he took over the business and, as it grew, Wall's products were regularly noted for their taste and quality and enjoyed by noted consumers, including the Royal household.

Summer caused problems for the business, as sales fell away due to the limited availability of refrigeration. In 1913, the business was run by Richard Wall's son Thomas and the idea to spread the company's turnover through the year by marketing ice cream was developed. World War I intervened, but in 1922 the Wall's sausage factory in Acton, West London, created its first ice cream department. It soon became clear that a different form of distribution was needed to that used successfully for the pies and sausages and Lionel Rodd developed the first Wall's tricycle in 1923. With crates of ice cream fitted onto tricycles, the sellers would hope that someone would stop them and buy one and eventually the tricycle-pushers became salesmen, stopping and knocking on doors.

According to a 1957 Wall's in-house journal, the idea behind these tri-cycle salesmen came when the then Managing Director, Mr Lionel Rodd observed a man selling bootlaces from a box on a tricycle and attracting customers by ringing a bell. The company soon built a tricycle (which is understood to have cost £6) and loaded its insulated box carrier with ice cream; Mr Cecil Rodd took the first trike on the road, followed by three weeks of trials, presumably in the Acton area. The conclusion was that the company could very well be onto a winner, and ten trikes were said to have been ordered for the summer season. The now famous slogan 'Stop Me And Buy One' was invented by Cecil Rodd and soon was displayed on the growing numbers of trikes pedalled by the 'Wallsie' salesmen. Later on Wall's distributed cards with a printed 'W', which were to be displayed in the house window whenever the 'Wallsie' man was required to call.

Using tricycles to deliver right to consumers' doors was an immediate success and in 1924 the salesmen were issued with uniforms, boots and caps in dark blue and white, with the tricycles painted dark blue. The 'Wallsie' man's day was arduous, for not only did he have to pedal up to 20 miles in his twelve-hour day, he also worked a seven-day week in the season, and a three-day week in the winter. To keep the trikes cold solid carbon dioxide was used to refrigerate the ice cream containers.

As the product became increasingly more popular, distribution depots were established and as the business started to expand a second ice cream department was set up in 1924 at the firm's sausage factory at Godley near Manchester. Having introduced dry ice as a cooling method, the Acton factory installed its own dry ice manufacturing unit in 1927, which significantly reduced costs across the business and also the weight of the tricycles. Through the 1920s, Wall's developed its first advertising campaigns, aiming to familiarise consumers with the ice cream and the brand name, by then part of the Unilever organisation.

Thomas Wall died in 1930 and was the last of the family dynasty, but the famous name continued. Three years later, in 1933, Acton was also expanded to include a wafer production facility. The 1930s saw a continued period of expansion, especially as the economy recovered from the Depression but dark clouds were on the horizon as Britain sizzled in consecutive record-breaking summers. The week after war was declared in September 1939, advertisements appeared saying: 'Keep cool! Keep calm! You can still buy your Ice Cream from the familiar Blue Tricycle' but the optimism didn't last.

In fact, before very long the tricycles were 'called up' into national service. Here they provided valuable 'war service' although never actually coming under fire, as they were used for Royal Air Force ground control training and distributing food to canteens at airfields, army camps and munitions factories. Some were used in radar experiments, and still others were handed over to the Post Master General, and they were then used for both GPO telegram and postal deliveries. Ice cream itself was impossible to obtain during World War II until its production was once more permitted in 1944.

Whereas before the war, Wall's sold about 90% of its ices via tricycles, in the post-war period about 90% was sold through shops and the landscape changed dramatically for what we now call ice cream mobiling. The introduction of vans instead of trikes combined with the post-war need for huge amounts of affordable housing and through the 1950s, pale blue and cream Wall's vans were a regular site around these new streets of the UK. The 'Stop Me and Buy One' slogan was set to music by the dance-band leader Peter Yorke, who composed the distinctive five-chime tune for Wall's mobiles.

In 1959, the decision was made to build a new ice cream factory and the site at Gloucester was chosen, which is still the home of Wall's ice cream production in the UK. Alongside the ice cream facility was a bakery to produce wafers and cones and Gloucester operated alongside the Acton factory until that closed in 1986.

1960s

In 1980, Unilever announced that it was to merge its ice cream and frozen food businesses in the UK, as had already been done successfully across Europe. Wall's merged with Birds Eye to become Birds Eye Wall's, which became Unilever Ice Cream & Frozen Food in March 2003.

Mr.Whippy and Wall's mobiling – by then franchised – went into decline through the 1980s, as 24-hour, seven-day trading became part of UK life and consumers acquired household freezers. The Wall's business changed as multi-packs supplied those home freezers and new channels opened up but mobiling remained an important way of bringing ice cream to consumers in their homes and when they were out and about. Despite the modern pressures, the original concept of making ice cream easy to find and enjoy continues to be important for Wall's.

1970s

At the start of 1989, Birds Eye Wall's brought a fresh approach to mobiling. A new yellow design came in, and was used until a new Heart logo brought consistency in the branding of Unilever's ice creams across Europe in January 1998. In 1996, the SenseStation was invented to bring to consumers at events around the UK some of the excitement of ice cream together with an insight into how it is created.

The new Heart logo and vibrant colours launched across Europe in March 2003 gave the Wall's Mobiling and Event division a whole new image, bringing fun and excitement back to ice cream in a way that will appeal to the consumers of the 21st Century. Mobiling also has a new shape, with the brand new Citroen Picasso vehicle complementing the more traditional ice cream vans. The Picasso will sell Cornetto Soft and impulse ice cream to consumers in places where larger vehicles are unable to go – a return to the ethos of the tricycles of 80 years ago.

1980s

The pictures on these two pages give a flavour, or time line, to the Wall's story and they set the scene for what will appear in our next book, due for launch at the 2004 Ice Cream Alliance Exhibition. Starting from the top left we see an advertising brochure from the early days, which features the Wall's ice cream salesman of the 1920s and 1930s; the next view is of a Model A Ford that was used to supply the company depots in the same era. By the end of World War II, the need for bigger and more durable delivery lorries was evident, and examples like this 5-ton Bedford O-Type were employed. The 1950s and '60s saw a boom in mobile ice cream vehicles, with vehicles like the Austin/Morris LD and the Ford Thames 307E becoming common sights. The Bedford CF and the Ford Transit were the main contenders in the 1970s and 1980s, and more recently the Transit has vied with the Mercedes Sprinter. Today the prominent body builder is Whitby of Crewe, a firm that has acquired both the Cummins and Morrison brands discussed in this book.

1990s

Of course the Wall's story continues to evolve under the direction of Unilever's Ice Cream & Frozen Food operation, and over the next year we will be working together to hopefully present the authorised biography of the Wall's fleet. This finished book is an example of that co-operation, and we hope that it will inspire readers to dig out their own memories on the various aspects of the Wall's operation. Whether the reader is a former company employee, a mobiler, or someone who simply enjoyed the great frozen confectionary that the firm produced, we would like to hear from them. These memories can be anecdotal or photographic, but they will help us as we produce the history of this great company and a very famous fleet. If you can help, please write to the author of that book; Alan Earnshaw, at Trans-Pennine Publishing Ltd. PO Box 10, Appleby-in-Westmorland, Cumbria. All loaned material will, of course, be promptly returned.

2000s

CONCLUSION

When soft ice cream first hit the streets way back in 1959, the public loved it and healthy sales would even continue through the long winter months. In modern times, it's much harder to make a living from mobiling and as a result no large company-owned fleets remain. Brands such as Wall's and Nestles would, I am sure, prefer to sell their quality controlled wrapped products from franchised mobiles, rather than 'Fluffy' soft-serve ice cream. However, the British do love their 'Mr.Whippy' and therefore both companies still promote a national franchised fleet of soft-serve mobiles

When posing the question of who were Mr.Whippy's competitors back in its heyday, it would be easy to point to brands such as Mister Softee. However, the real answer to this question has to be any mobiler working the same streets as Mr.Whippy. In fact, independent mobilers and small fleet operators probably outnumbered the big boys and quickly fought back by converting their hard vans, or by purchasing new soft vans from companies such as Cummins of Crewe. In conclusion, it is well worth remembering, that although Mr.Whippy and Mister Softee had a great national brand image, it was, and still is, the small dedicated ice cream manufacturer that regularly win all those coveted Gold or Silver medals!

Above: *Although no longer actively marketed by Unilever Ice Cream Foods, the Mr.Whippy name still continues strongly in some parts. Looking very smart in her embroidered 'Mrs.Whippy' uniform, Margaret Donovan takes great pride in her Mrs.Whippy van. She was recently nominated for mobiler of the year 2003.*

With Acknowledgement

Ice Cream Alliance	Leslie Edwards	Pim Reinders
John Adams	Stan Gordon	Matt Richardson
Mike Allen	Lisa Green	Hilary Robertson
Aztec Oils Ltd	Jock Gwilt	Karl Rozzo
Andy Ballisat	Peter Hopkins	Terry Shaw
Joan Barras	John James	Shell UK
Jennie Bell	Kevin Jennings	Colin Tarr
Stan Buchan	Brian Lilley	Kathryn Taylor
Antonio Catalano	Michael Lloyd	Ian & Nick Smith
Geoff Caverhill	Keith Metcalf	Bob Staff
Denise Conklin	Howard Mitchel	Robby Staff
Richard Conklin	Terry Newman	Jim Valenti
Kevin Donovan	Brent Owen	Burt Williams
Margaret Donovan	Anthony Pacitto	Robin Weir
John Duke	Melanie Peart	Stuart Whitby
Alan Earnshaw	Steve Pheasant	Jean Yates